D1522794

Digging through History Again

Digging through History Again

New Discoveries from Atlantis to the Holocaust

Richard A. Freund

ROWMAN & LITTLEFIELD
Lanham · Boulder · New York · London

Published by Rowman & Littlefield
An imprint of The Rowman & Littlefield Publishing Group, Inc.
4501 Forbes Boulevard, Suite 200, Lanham, Maryland 20706
www.rowman.com

86-90 Paul Street, London EC2A 4NE

British Library Cataloguing in Publication Information Available

Library of Congress Cataloging-in-Publication Data

ISBN 978-1-5381-3622-5 (cloth : alk. paper)
ISBN 978-1-5381-3623-2 (electronic)

∞™ The paper used in this publication meets the minimum requirements of American
National Standard for Information Sciences—Permanence of Paper for Printed Library
Materials, ANSI/NISO Z39.48-1992.

To Bert Aaron, whose legacy will continue to inspire us!

Contents

Acknowledgments

There are many more acknowledgments that I have to make since the 2012 publication of *Digging through History*. As the Bertram and Gladys Aaron Professor of Jewish Studies at Christopher Newport University in Newport News, Virginia, I have to thank the administration and staff at CNU, including President Paul Trible, Provost Dave Doughty, Dean Lori Underwood, Sponsored Project Director Anne Pascucci, Research Director David Salomon, and Study Abroad Director Mandi Pierce, who all welcomed our geoscience and archaeology projects at CNU. Our work has now expanded to include Lithuania, Latvia, Poland, and Greece, and the reception that the university has accorded our group has been rewarding. Bertram and Gladys Aaron, donors of the endowed chair I hold, have been new sponsors of my work and the passing of Bertram in 2022 was a great loss for the university and for me personally. In the past decade, our projects' films have emanated from our students and from directors around the world. They include two student documentary projects directed by my colleague Professor Susan Cardillo at the University of Hartford (*Finding Matilda* and *Secrets of the Great Synagogue*), French Lithuanian director Loic Salfati (*The Great Synagogue and Shulhoyf of Vilna*), Lithuanian director Ruta Vyzintaite (*Tales from the Depths of the Lagoon*), Israeli Canadian director Simcha Jacobovici working with the American director James Cameron (*Atlantis Rising*), Israeli Yaron Niski and Canadian Ric Esther Bienstock (*The Good Nazi*), US-based directors Kirk Wolfinger and Paula Apsell (*Holocaust Escape Tunnel*), and in production *Resistance: They Fought Back!*). In this same time period our team has published thirty articles and conference papers. Many of these publications included students as coauthors, and I have worked with archaeologists, museum directors, and geoscientists from many countries who have followed our work and methodology quite closely.

In particular, I want to thank Rabbi Michael Schudrich, rabbinical leader in Warsaw, Dr. Albert Stankowski and Dr. Jacek Konik of the Warsaw Ghetto Museum; Markas Zingeris, Jurate Razumiene, Zigmas Vitkus, Irina Guzenberg, and Mantas Siksnianas of the Vilna Gaon Jewish State Museum and Ponar Museum; and the director of the Rhodes Jewish Museum, Carmen Cohen. At Auschwitz I want to personally thank Dr. Piotr Cywinski, director of the Auschwitz Memorial, who met with us in Kansas City in June 2021 and allowed us to film and work at Auschwitz in August, and Pawel Sawicki, head of the Press Office of the Auschwitz Memorial, who worked with us in August 2021. At the Rokiskis regional museum, I am grateful to Marijona Mieliauskiene, the museum's deputy director, and Giedrius Kujelis, the director of the Museum's History Department. At Fort IX Museum, I thank director Marius Pečiulis and the head of the History Department, Vytautas Petrikenas, and their staff for graciously providing us with access to the museum, its archives, and the areas of investigation around the museum. Finally, my thanks go to the archaeological staff at the Great Synagogue of and Shulhoyf Project in Vilna, including Zenonas Baubonis, Jon Seligman, Justinas Racas, and Mantas Daubaras; at Fort IX, Gintautas Zabielas; at HKP 562, Ramounas Smigelkas; and at Rokiskis, Romas Jarokas. In Poland, Director Tomasz Kranz from the new Sobibor and Majdanek museums and archaeologists, Yoram Haimi and Wojciech Mazureck at Sobibor and Gary Hochman, documentarian.

Our funding sponsors for the geoscience work included the US Embassy in Lithuania and the US Embassy in Latvia, the US Commission for the Preservation of America's Heritage Abroad in Washington, D.C., including our first contacts there, Joan Silber and Barbi Broadus. Our other funders included William Freund, I. Martin Pompadur, the Targum Shelishi Foundation, and the Smart Family Fund as well as our own universities.

This is a book about history and the writing of history, but it is not a history book. This is also a book about archaeology and how archaeological research contributes to our understanding of history, but it is not an archaeology textbook. It is a book about the major issues and mysteries of how religion and religious faiths interact in history, but it is not a religious handbook. Mostly this is a book about my own encounter with topics from the beginnings of civilization at Atlantis to the near end of civilization during the Holocaust.

Over the past thirty years I have collected the results of research projects that I have participated in and which I feel add to the understanding of history and archaeology. The book is written for the general public and interested readers, rather than trained historians, scholars of religion, theologians, or archaeologists. This is an introductory-level book on how archaeology can help us understand history better when we track how archaeological work has enlightened us in a few key periods over the past four thousand years. I have chosen a number of examples that I have firsthand knowledge of, and I include a bibliography at the end of the book for the reader to peruse. I allude to many of the different views held by others about each event or site. While I attempt to bring in some of the other major theories on some of these sites, I present my own theories and information from sites of which that I have had first-hand knowledge. I did not start out twenty-five years ago intending to write this book. It began to take shape gradually as my own interests and research in the history of the world and Jewish history began to coalesce. Over the past decade, I have just begun to notice over time that I was teaching and researching in different time periods and the chapters parallel my own research and scholarly presentations at professional societies. The fact that I am able to write a book with the title *Digging through History Again: New Discoveries from Atlantis to the Holocaust* is largely because I "stand on the shoulders" of many teachers and pioneers in different disciplines of research and because in each project I was working with a group of specialists who allowed me to participate in their research.

The ideas in the chapters of this book have been presented at professional conferences of the American Academy or Religion, the Association of Jewish Studies, the Society of Biblical Literature (regional, national, and international conferences), and the American Schools of Oriental Research over the past thirty years. I am thankful for the feedback I received at these conferences. This book is intended for nonspecialists in archaeology, religion, history, and biblical studies and is not intended to take the place of the more academic tomes that are also available.

Any errors that have occurred in the reporting of the data in this book are my responsibility alone. The ideas presented here, however, are based on data that I, as well as other scholars, have collected, lectured on, presented at conferences, and published. All the information I used in the book was reported to me either orally or in writing through interim reports, lectures, and conferences in geology, geography, religion, history, and archaeology.

WRITING ABOUT ARCHAEOLOGY FOR THE PUBLIC

This volume, like *Digging through the Bible* (Rowman & Littlefield, 2009) and my book *Secrets of the Cave of Letters* (Prometheus, 2004), and even our four volumes on *Bethsaida: A City by the North Shore of the Sea of Galilee* (Truman State University, 1995, 1999, 2004, 2009) follows a precedent that was started by Yigael Yadin in the 1960s (in Hebrew and later in English) in books on Hazor, Masada, and Bar Kokhba. They contain archaeological data researched by scholars but written primarily for the general public. Not every historian can effectively negotiate archaeological data, especially when there are religious texts that are affected by the assessments, and not every archaeologist can write history, especially when it comes to religious texts. It is even more difficult to write about both for the general public. One of the best examples of how it can be done is found in exhibition catalogs. In the exhibition catalog *Searching for Ancient Egypt: Art, Architecture and Artifacts* (Dallas Museum of Art/University of Pennsylvania, 1997), Egyptologist, Donald Redford writes: ["Following the close of Dynasty 12 (nineteenth century BCE)] . . . long-standing commercial links with Byblos on the Phoenician coast resulted in the establishment of an emporium of Asiatic merchants at Avaris in the eastern Delta, and this eventually became the base for a violent takeover by an Asiatic regime, which, around the middle of the seventeenth century B.C.E., established itself in the Delta (Dynasty 15, called by the Egyptians "foreign rulers," or Hyksos. Settlements whose inhabitants displayed Middle Bronze IIb culture of Palestine sprang up along the eastern fringe of the Delta." Redford nowhere mentions the Bible, but his writing has incorporated elements from stories of the Patriarchs and Matriarchs of the Bible, the Exodus, and the excavations of over one hundred years in the Delta, Avaris, and the Nile valley south of what is today Cairo. Without footnotes, with limited archaeological jargon, he presents a complex history for an audience which fully understands the subtext. His assessment tells the "informed" reader about how the familiar Bible fits in with historical data gleaned from archaeology.

These types of books and exhibition catalogs (see the bibliography in the back for many others) have engaged the general public in thinking about the Bible, history, and archaeological data that has been uncovered in the past half century in a serious and informed way. This book is different from the other books I have read in that it includes a critical methodology of the Bible and history, covers the different biblical periods, and continues its trajectory into the modern period. It raises most of the major questions asked my students and by participants in lectures around the country. Also unlike other works, this book covers topics within each of the different historical periods from the beginning of civilization until the "almost end" of civilization in the Holocaust (I calculate almost five thousand years), and it does not begin with the Bible, but rather with a question from outside but parallel to the rise of civilization in the Middle East–Atlantis. That is the main reason I called it

Digging through History. It is a continuation of the book I published in 2009, *Digging through the Bible*, *Digging through History* (2012), and *Archaeology of the Holocaust* (2019), but it goes beyond the Bible and covers different sites and a much wider swath of human history than just biblical history.

Richard A. Freund
Bertram and Gladys Aaron Professor of Jewish Studies
Christopher Newport University
Newport News, VA

The Archaeology of Atlantis

Searching for the Atlantis Civilization 2010–2022

> Yet, before proceeding further in the narrative, I ought to warn you, that you must not be surprised if you should perhaps hear Hellenic names given to foreigners. I will tell you the reason of this: Solon, who was intending to use the tale for his poem, enquired into the meaning of the names, and found that the early Egyptians in writing them down had translated them into their own language, and he recovered the meaning of the several names and when copying them out again translated them into our language. My great-grandfather, Dropides, had the original writing, which is still in my possession, and was carefully studied by me when I was a child.
>
> —Plato, *Critias*[1]

We did not go out looking for Atlantis. We were invited to add our expertise to the developing work being done in Spain in the early 2000s and followed up on that work. This is the follow-up. Our geoscience group was invited to Spain to perform surveys in 2008–2009 during an ongoing Hinojos Project in the southern marsh known as Doña Ana. We started from the studies of the Spanish team as well as with information from Plato's geographical literary information. Where was Atlantis located according to Plato? Not in Greece but in an area that was known to most Greeks—the so-called Pillars of Hercules, a site now known as the Strait of Gibraltar. What was Plato describing? Not pottery but monumental and unique architecture and land-scapes, minerals, animals, and agriculture that can be tracked. We take our literary sources seriously but not literally. We started from the premise that if there once was an Atlantis, there must have been artifacts, architecture, and other evidence that would have survived despite the catastrophic end of the city described by Plato. More important, Plato had to rely upon the fact that his ancient Greek readers both knew the story of Atlantis and would see the details of his account as meaningful. He must have worried that Athens might suffer the same end as Atlantis, and was certainly using Atlantis as a metaphor. For the metaphor to work, however, it must have credibility as a

Map of our research in southern Spain. (Courtesy of Philip Reeder, Duquesne University)

physical site in order to make the comparison between Athens and Atlantis valid. Yes, his use of Atlantis's rise and demise are attempts to teach the Athenians a thing or two about their possible fate. But he had to know that his Greek readers saw the story as real.

My biggest question was how a story from thousands of years before Plato persisted into his own time. Even given the timeline that Plato suggests via the traditions maintained in his family from the time of Solon to the fourth century BCE, the account goes back thousands of years before Solon. I think that the active memory of the Atlantis civilization persisted through to the fourth century BCE because it was so powerful as a story and because the innovations and characteristics of the original city were recreated in a number of port cities in the Mediterranean. Atlantis was memorialized in both Spain and throughout the Mediterranean for thousands of years after it was destroyed because many of its architectural, artifactual, and aesthetic characteristics were incorporated into cities that shared what I call the Atlantis civilization effect. The memory of the Atlantis civilization was preserved in Spain in memorial or ritual villages, but it was also preserved at port cities throughout the Mediterranean Sea. In places like the Azores, Carthage, Sardinia, Sicily, Malta, Morocco, Tunisia, and elsewhere in the Mediterranean, traders and survivors of the destruction of the original Atlantis created

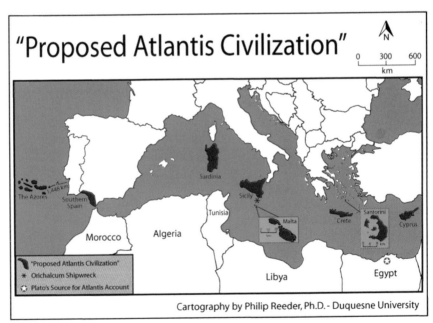

Map of Atlantis Civilization. (Courtesy of Philip Reeder, Duquesne University)

versions of the Atlantis port through a mimicking of architecture and culture that both remembered the ancient Atlantis and added details that may or may not have been present in the original Atlantis. The memory of architecture, artifacts, and decorations of Atlantis continued right up until at least the seventh century BCE, when an Athenian statesman, Solon, who had heard the story for the first time in Egypt, visited the site. It was a mere three hundred years of oral transmission through his family to Critias, who told the story to Plato. The story of Atlantis was first passed down through the port cities that memorialized the ancient city and then was passed down to the time of Critias and Plato. It is an epic tale, but it did not only inspire ancient Greeks and Romans. It continues to inspire people in our own time. For me, in this new revised version of *Digging through History*, I wanted to share new insights that I have about how memory is preserved in archaeology. The story of Atlantis did not end in Spain. It began in Spain and continued for millennia outside of Spain. That is what brought us back to Spain in 2016 and again in 2020, this last time to the dunes by the ocean, to search for the evidence of the Atlantis civilization both in and out of Spain.

WERE THERE MULTIPLE ATLANTISES?

For this revision of *Digging through History*, I decided to update readers on our follow-up research in southern Spain in 2016 and 2020. I suggest that before you read this chapter you read the original chapter of *Digging through History* on Atlantis again. It is still as groundbreaking as it was in 2011 when I finished it. In May 2016, we returned to the question of Atlantis's location with a new question: *Were there multiple Atlantises?*

Of the thousands of letters I received following the worldwide 2011 screening of *Finding Atlantis* there were of four different types. There were those writers who congratulated us in presenting a plausible theory. There were those letters written by researchers who raised certain inconsistencies in our research design that I read with great interest. There were letters from professional and nonprofessional researchers who wanted to know more but cited research from far-flung areas in their own geographic locations (from Asia to South America) that immediately seemed unlikely. Most of these were sent by nonprofessionals, but some included a very extensive research study naming Bolivia, a land-locked South American country, as Atlantis. Finally, there was also a group of letters from researchers who placed their Atlantis in the Mediterranean but not in Spain. During 2012–2015 I corresponded with some of these researchers to understand more about their sites. One of the consistent themes was a location in sedimented areas that had some access to the Mediterranean in antiquity but now had none. They illustrated their articles with photos and maps, and it all led me to question our own work in southern Spain. Plato describes the southern plain of Atlantis as being three thousand by two thousand stadia in size, which equals in square miles less than the state of Nebraska that I was familiar with. Plato also describes mountain ranges and mining areas that are unique and would have made the area only possible in North Africa or Europe (or he is describing a massive place to inspire his readers' sense of awe). Even assuming a less-than-awe-inspiring land mass, I realized that none of the existing islands in the Mediterranean fit the criteria, although I did take seriously proposals that included Morocco, Tunisia, and Egypt. Other letters started me to consider that there might be some relationship between the different sites even when they did not fulfill all of the criteria. I knew, for example, that there were port cities along the Mediterranean Sea and into the Atlantic Ocean that possessed an Atlantis-like construction of nested concentric walls in places, such as Carthage, Sardinia, Malta, and even in the Azores. They were all, it seems, later than the construction in southern Spain, and they all were lacking the other features present in Plato's description. One particular researcher was quite insistent that his location, Tunisia, fit the size (as does the area of southern Spain). One of the missed ideas is that the Mediterranean Sea itself was reshaped in the Bronze Age through seismic activity. This researcher wrote me about the possibility that the Pillars of Hercules were identified in different periods in different locations. The idea that the Pillars of Hercules was located between Sicily and Tunisia and the original Tunisian Atlantis was inland or on the altered eastern coastline is the substance of many different studies and was one of the reasons that I continued in contact with this researcher. In 2012 to 2015, this researcher sent a series of emails based upon his own field studies near Lake Tritonis, a dried-up saltwater lake known as Chott el Jerid in Tunisia. It had been considered earlier by researchers in the nineteenth and twentieth centuries, but it is such a massive location that only with our geophysical equipment could we confirm the existence of buried city walls in the barren salt flats. The researcher I was corresponding with had narrowed the site down to a very specific location outside of Gafsa. He carried out field study in the region of Gafsa, namely Alsarragiya, in the area around Mount Bouramli in the northwest of Gafsa. The site was massive even by Plato's scale, and it rivaled southern Spain with the tectonic events that had scarred the area. It was included on a short list of places that we were going to visit in 2016 to explore my idea of why there might be multiple "Atlantises." Months before the expedition to explore these different sites was planned in 2016 the researcher in Tunisia passed away, and speaking to his children on the phone, I sense the pain in their voices. He had devoted decades to his research and now they feared there would be no follow-up.

While there are those who would say that the idea of multiple Atlantises is impossible (that there can only be one Atlantis, one Athens, one Jerusalem, or one Tenochtitlan), I started to think about the issue differently. After reviewing scores of sites and looking at the evidence from researchers who held that their site was Atlantis in those locations, I started to conclude that either the people at these locations had planned their own sites as "copycat" sites (similar to franchises) or that Atlantis was more than just a singular city in a singular location in a singular time period. Atlantis was more than just a city; it was an idea that had a historical starting point but gave rise to other versions of the city in the period after the destruction of the original island/city, and it was because the idea was so persuasive that it persisted for hundreds and later thousands of years after its demise. "Atlantis" was the spread of culture, architecture, and a real "civilization," and this concept required a broader vision of Atlantis, one that rivaled Athens in the mind of Plato. I was convinced by the thousands of letters that I received from all over the world that Atlantis was more than the sum of the parts mentioned in Plato. My main questions to each of these researchers were always the same. They had read my book and seen the documentary, so we had a common point of departure:

1. How do their sites more faithfully parallel the details of Plato's narratives than the sites I had worked on in southern Spain?
2. Are there any support cities in and around their island/port site that parallel the ancient support and memorial cities that we had been researching in and around our southern Spain site?
3. How old are the other sites they are researching, and how was the site age determined?
4. What artifacts do the other sites have that the southern Spain site and its supporting cities do not have?
5. How do they account for the continued existence of their site and the completely destroyed nature of the Atlantis site in the writings of Plato?

Many of the champions of other sites simply could not answer most of my questions with any level of scientific accuracy and ultimately, were only able to demonstrate similarities to the site as described by Plato. Most were at least as old as the Iron Age (1200 BCE or so), but in most of the cases the city in question was not destroyed; it was still standing in plain sight. This disqualification of sorts was my first clue that these other sites might be related to the original site of Atlantis but were later versions of the city.

These were not like the memorial cities we had found in the central part of Spain (Cancho Roano and La Mata, for example), but were thriving ancient cities. They reminded me of the relationship between the medieval port city of "Amsterdam" in the Netherlands and the port city of "New Amsterdam" in what became New York. The existence of these other, later but still ancient port/cities, in the case of Atlantis, however, indirectly bolstered my argument and gave meaning to the research that many of these people had done. If there were "copycat" cities in a later period, it implied that there must have been a more ancient model that they were basing themselves on. Their structures may be later, but they were in many ways taking the civilization of Atlantis on the road and making it possible for the whole ancient story to be recorded in the time of Plato, long after the ancient Atlantis was gone from the stage of history.

To test this theory of the Atlantis civilization, I did two different types of research. First, I chose a series of places where there was enormous evidence, and this became the *Atlantis Rising* documentary in 2016 when Simcha Jacobovici went to these places and talked to the researchers I was corresponding with (on camera). I recommended sites such as Santorini, Sardinia, Malta, the Azores, and even other sites in Tunisia, Libya, and Morocco that had been built to purposely resemble the original Atlantis and thus are part of what I call the larger and later Atlantis civilization. Under normal circumstances a researcher at each location would have spent their lives devoted to that individual site and not see the bigger picture. Simcha Jacobovici is really an investigative journalist with a keen eye for the "big picture." He wanted to talk to each researcher himself and present their arguments in the best way that he could: in film. He was genuinely committed to seeking out the story behind the story of Atlantis in southern Spain.

My theory is dependent upon the locations of much more evidence in Spain, near the site of Doña Ana, which would have been what I call support cities. In every major site there have to be other, smaller, similarly dated sites to support the activities of the larger city. In Spain, our agenda was twofold: first to look seriously at the many researchers that had written to me about their own "Atlantis" sites and second, to engage with one of the most productive researchers on the "Atlantis in Spain" theory, Georgeos Díaz-Montexano (see his chapter below). Our 2016 and 2020 projects were based again upon Georgeos's quarter century of research on Atlantis in Spain and Schulten and Bonsor's work almost one hundred years earlier. The other half of the work was the accumulated information sent to me starting in 2011.

The search for the Atlantis civilization started with the unique architecture of Atlantis that is found in the writings and is a sine qua non for the locations outside and inside Spain. The three "nested" walls of a stone structure, together with concentric circles or banks of land and sea or land and water (moat-like) as a guide was one of the major pointers for our work. In Spain and in the Mediterranean, we were looking for an island or land (that disappeared under these cataclysmic circumstances) near Plato's travel locations from Athens. We included areas of investigation in Italy, Sicily, Malta, Morocco, Egypt, Sardinia, Crete, Cyprus, and the depths of the Aegean Sea.

With the beginnings of systematic archaeology at the end of the nineteenth century, many ancient mysteries were researched in the twentieth century in this area. Atlantis was at the top of the list. After work began at a site thought to be ancient Troy, Atlanteologists looked for Atlantis in and around Troy or at the bottom of the Black Sea. Plato's descriptions of the technological advances of Atlantis seemed miraculous in the ancient world, so some speculated that Atlantis might have been located near the site of other miracle stories in Egypt and the Sinai Peninsula. Others held that the tale originated with an ancient civilization on the coast of India or Indonesia where the environmental conditions described by Plato were more common. In these locations, tsunamis and volcanoes regularly crushed cities and submerged whole islands. This is an area of two or three different fault systems under the water, which inevitably made them earthquake-prone areas as well. By the twentieth century, the beginnings of marine archaeology placed Atlantis off the coasts of the Iberian Peninsula, especially in southern Spain and Portugal (where the remnants of the ancient land masses could be found on the ocean floor). But others speculated that Atlantis may have sunk off the coast of northern Spain, or in the Irish Sea, the North Sea, the Mediterranean Sea, or even in the Atlantic Ocean. Even though it is clear that Plato related stories passed on to him from Europe, Asia, and Africa (and not North or South America), that did not stop speculation in the twentieth century that the location of Atlantis could be found in the Japan, Bahamas, Cuba, Mexico, and even landlocked Bolivia.

I have been most convinced by those who have actually done field research, especially when I consider the prospect of moving Plato's scenario to southern Morocco, interior Tunisia, Malta, the Azores, and Sardinia. For reasons of security we were unable to research every one of the sites that I thought were relevant, but I was happy that I had so many researchers in the world willing to share their research. Two of them, one in Tunisia and one in Morocco, died before I was able to work with them. Many other European researchers placed Atlantis in areas in and around Denmark, Finland, Sweden, Greenland, Iceland, and even Antarctica because these were areas they were most familiar with. Since they usually took Plato as being purely literary and not historical in the least, they placed the "Pillars of Hercules" in a variety of locations and only looked for some of the architectural features or the example of a lost island. In short, for some, speculation on the location of Atlantis meant that it could be anywhere.

We started with the Plato geographical information. Where was Atlantis located, according to Plato? Not in his backyard but rather at the "Pillars of Hercules" which is now known as the Strait of Gibraltar. What was Plato describing? Not pottery, but rather, monumental architecture, even though to get a picture of the sites we must find what type of pottery and what type of details of daily life they are describing. I also started from the premise that there must be a series of trademark-like artifacts and illustrations that would have survived. It is hard to destroy all of the evidence from around a single site even in light of the cataclysmic events.

In my opinion, you must take the details of Plato's work seriously even if you think that his major reason for writing the *Timaeus* and *Critias* was to critique Athens in his own time. When I read the 1950s Arthur Miller play, *The Crucible,* for example, I know that the content of play is about seventeenth-century witch trials in Salem, Massachusetts, and that it relies upon the firsthand knowledge that Americans had of those trials as a part of American history. He included details of the life and times of the Puritans to make it extremely accurate. Most readers, however, knew that it was really was a barely hidden critique of the 1950s Communist witch trials that were going on in Washington, D.C., that Miller was analyzing through the lens of the story of Salem. In order for Miller to write an impactful piece, he had to rely upon the fact that the readers knew both the original Salem story and what was going on in Washington in their own time. So too Plato had to rely upon the fact that his readers both knew the story of Atlantis and its details and the story of Athens as it was unfolding in his own time. How had the story of Atlantis persisted in the active consciousness of the people of Athens even before Plato's writings? I think through the active memory of the Atlantis civilization that continued right up until his own time, understanding it to be a network of ancient cities and ports on the Mediterranean that continued to memorialize the ancient city both actively and passively in their landscapes and perhaps even in an ancient dialect that they continued to perpetuate. That is what brought us back to Spain in 2016 and again in 2020, this last time I worked in the dunes by the ocean.

THE FOUR LINES OF EVIDENCE FOR THE ATLANTIS CIVILIZATION THAT BEGAN IN SOUTHERN SPAIN

In order to understand what the Atlantis civilization is, I will start with the evidence that we have assembled. There are various lines of evidence that, while different in nature, contribute to our understanding of how the theory advanced above was developed. The four lines of evidence are:

1. Literary and historical textual evidence
2. Geographical evidence
3. Geological evidence
4. Archaeological evidence

Literary and Historical Evidence

The first literary question has to do with whether we have a credible textual tradition or not. Plato is a pretty good source and the manuscript tradition of Plato's works is reliable (even though it looks like something happened to the second part of the *Critias* that just ends in the middle of a thought). Plato's thirty-nine dialogues and other works sit in the canon of Western civilization, yet it is hard to have him accepted as a credible source. Even as we read Plato seriously we rarely read him uncritically. Generations of Plato scholars have investigated the diverse types of writing, vocabulary, readings, and even the style of Plato's writings. It is not that we do not read Plato critically; there are people who do. But not everyone who uses Plato knows that there is whole tradition of reading his writing using critical modern linguistic and literary analysis. I contend that we must read Plato seriously but not literally. I have had Plato scholars tell me that the *Timaeus* and the *Critias* are moral tales that only relate to events from Plato's own time. This idea of a moral tale from Plato's time actually gives the storyline of the ancient Atlantis greater authenticity, rather than less.

The nine-thousand-year-old question is: "When was the original Atlantis founded?" If you pressed me for a date, I would say approximately 4000 BCE. This revision chapter is also intended to answer some of the questions that people asked me about over the years that I thought needed a more detailed answer. Some researchers have asked me how we can even start with a site that is "only" some six thousand years old since Plato specifically says "nine thousand years" before his own time. I have an answer to that critique that is related to the nature of ancient writing and texts in general.

This is where a good grasp of ancient texts and dating can help. I tell students that I take Plato *seriously* but not literally. This literary point often confuses well-meaning scientific researchers who simply do not understand the nature of ancient writing. For ancient writers who employ times and chronologies at all (most ancient writers do not) the use of an ancient number or year was not intended to do anything other than give general parameters. Therefore, "9,000" is decidedly not the number after "8,999"—it is a literary convention that seems to indicate "a very, very long time ago." It is the date that Plato uses for the founding of the city, but it is just a Greek literary convention for a very ancient period.

When we read ancient texts as "modern" we tend to literalize them. In antiquity, the reader would understand it as it was intended—that is, "Once upon a time." Since long chronological time was simply incalculable in antiquity, all ancient writers had to employ expressions that would be understood by the readers in antiquity as indicating relative ancient chronological time sequencing. Some writers did want you to know that event "X" happened before event "Y." They used numbers as a handy way of expressing relative-relational time but not exact time. The numbers and combinations differ in different cultures. In ancient Chinese literature, a Chinese writer would employ numbers significant to the Chinese reader. So, for example, Chinese writers saw the numbers and sequences of 6, 8, and 9 as "lucky" or auspicious and might employ them to make a point. But an ancient Chinese writer also knew that the numbers 4 and 7 are seen as "unlucky" or inauspicious and would employ them to make another point. It is not just an ancient convention but is seen as in sync with some ancient timing gauge that is lost in the mists of local custom and sound. Among Hindus, Buddhists, and Jains, the number 108 has a similar significance of *completeness* and *wholeness*, and in Greek literature the number 9 seems to hold that same type of significance for ancient Greek writers and readers. The numbers 90, 900, and 9,000 would be manifestations of attempting to put an event into the very ancient mists of time.

The authors of the ancient Hebrew Bible, for example, employed a similar device when they wrote about the ancient flood in Genesis that lasted "40 days and 40 nights," but subsequently reveal in other chapters that the flood lasted for over a year. When we read that Moses was on Mount Sinai in the biblical book of Exodus for "40 days and 40 nights" receiving the Ten Commandments, it is clear that the numbers are a placeholder that simply means "a long time." When the Bible states that the Israelites were in the desert "40 years" or in Egypt for "400" years, these are really expressions of the same principle: "a long time" and "a very long time." The number 40 is the biblical language convention for a "long time" and 400 means a "very long time." This understanding of the symbolic meaning of the numbers can prevent archaeologists from becoming fundamentalists in looking for evidence in a particular time period based on literary conventions.

The nine thousand years of the ancient history of the creation of Atlantis is to be understood this way in Plato. In similar fashion, the Greeks, especially in the tradition of Homer and Hesiod, used the number 9 as their culturally significant number of choice. The *nine* Greek Muses show up in the canon of the literature early on. We read that Leto, the mother of Apollo, labored for *nine* days and *nine* nights before giving birth to him, or that Demeter searched for her missing daughter in all of the earth for *nine* days and *nine* nights, or we learn that the distance between Heaven and Earth is *the nine days and nine nights* that an anvil takes to land from there to here. The many uses of the "nine" reference make it plain that a learned Greek like Plato would have employed "9,000" to show that the founding of Atlantis happened "a very, very long time ago." Unfortunately, very good scientists read this text in Plato literally and become confused about whether any of the text has credibility. We must read ancient texts seriously, critically, but not literally.

Geographical Evidence

The second line of evidence is geographical. When Plato says that the event happened at the Pillars of Hercules, it is clear that he is writing about a well-known location in his own time. Herodotus and mariners in the Iron Age all the way through Ptolemy the second-century geographer knew exactly where the Pillars of Hercules were and placed them at the present-day Strait of Gibraltar. Although I can imagine that there were other places that may also be associated with the Pillars of Hercules (Hercules had many ancient tasks), in the Mediterranean area they were not called the *Pillars of Hercules* in the time of Plato. Some researchers literally moved the Pillars of Hercules to many different locations that would have been difficult for anyone with knowledge of the region in antiquity. None compare with the geographical tradition of that which we call the *Strait of Gibraltar* today. It is hard to move a site that was precisely identified in such a particular time period to give the reader of Plato's time a link to the site to give it greater credibility. It would be as if a modern author writing about 9/11 would place the site in a well-known location such as New York City and someone would attempt to locate New York City in Florida. The story is powerful because people had heard of the Atlantis story in the time of Plato and knew exactly where it was. Not only because Plato was telling them the story but because the story had been preserved in every major port city from Athens to the Azores. It was preserved in the tell-tale concentric walls and often artifacts.

Geological Evidence

The third line of evidence is from the geological work that has been done on the southern Spanish Doña Ana Park. Thanks to the remarkable work of the Hinojos Project team, we now know that there were many micro and macro-tsunamis that plagued an ancient Cadiz bay that extended from Cadiz to Seville in the Chalcolithic and early Bronze Age and that the bay was slowly closed off starting from the Iron Age onward. These micro- and macro-tsunamis accompanied by earthquakes and sedimentation from the rivers flowing to the ocean caused a catastrophic subsidence and earthquakes in a way that parallels the story of Atlantis in Plato and is not paralleled by any of the other sites. It is not easy to have so many geological conditions, "mud" "subsidence" and "sudden"coincide in an area that is defined by its proximity to the Pillars of Hercules. The Hinojos Project looked at eleven core sites from the northwest of the Hinojos area of the marsh to the southeast corner and it is clear that below the site, at a depth of up to thirteen meters, were massive amounts of organic matter sealed in a sudden catastrophic event somewhere after 2000 BCE. The cores and the C14-dated materials show an active site from 4000 BCE. The life of what was there extended over two thousand years. This is really more than just geological evidence. It is also what we use to understand the archaeological record in the sedimented bay.

Archaeological Evidence

What can radio-carbon dating, methane, and artifacts tell us about dating Atlantis? The core samples that were tested for C-14 dating are an important part of the process of the archaeology. Because we cannot generally do systematic excavations in the mud and sediments, the taking of C14 became a surrogate for the actual excavations. As you look at Figure 1.3 from north to south you can see the dating moves from very ancient BP (Before Present) to around 5000–4000 BP as you move southward in the marsh. This would entail the movement of thousands of pounds of materials from the center of the marsh to the edge of the sea. The methane layer would require those elements to be stuck together in a very concentrated area. The trapping of finds in an ancient tsunami event is key to the identification of any work in a place where an ancient site might have existed. If there was a massive ancient city with stone walls that were destroyed by an ancient tsunami, it will have remains in the nearby sea and should still have remains inside of the sedimented territory. The question is where to look and whether we can find anything to look at. In surveying the Doña Ana Park, we found one very good site to look for remains, a place where massive remains had already been found: Cerro del Trigo. It is south of the methane layer and it is hemmed in by two different dune sections that protected whatever was deposited there.

In the 2012 *Digging through History*, Figure 2.4 tells a story of all of the archaeology. The map of the tsunamis' line of destruction ends in the dune that protected the Cerro del Trigo site. From the north of this map you see R1, where the ceramics were found that we culturally labeled as "Phoenician-like," and then moving south to S1 is the area of the C14 samples, S4 where the wood sample was found at a depth of 13.5 meters, and finally the S8 layer of methane that to my mind tells us not only the direction of the tsunamis but tells us why the entire area is so sedimented in. The tsunamis blanketed the area with sediments that had no place to go. Only in an area where you have multiple tsunamis and earthquakes can you have a deposit as large and as specifically located as you find in this area.[2]

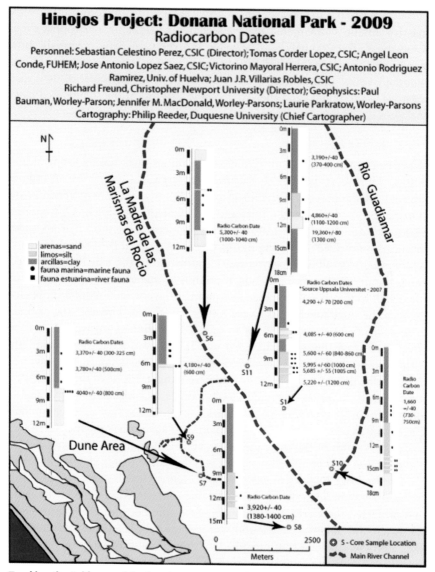

Tracking the Evidence of Ancient Mega-Tsunamis by tracking the C-14 cores. (Courtesy of Philip Reeder, Duquesne University)

Cerro del Trigo contains a 10-foot-long, 4.5-foot-thick, and 1-foot-high stone wall (i.e., above ground; the height extends at least 3 more feet below ground) section embedded in an excavation site dug by Bonsor and Schulten in the 1920s. It is still there. If there were massive stone outcroppings in the area, it would not be unique. But there are no stone outcroppings in the area, and it is clear that the very heavy material was deposited there and reused to create the wall section, which is located in the sand. It is perhaps one of the greatest discoveries of all time that no one knows about. To their credit, Spanish archaeologists over the past century have left it open and surrounded it with a small wooden fence. It has never been filled in by subsequent excavations in the area, perhaps because most realize the significance of the location. Cerro del Trigo stands in the center of the transgressive dune systems that now block access to the original rivers that made it a fishing and salting industry town from the second to the sixth century CE. The process of catching, salting, and shipping fish in the Roman Empire was big business, and this stable area of the dunes in the second century made the location desirable for the production of the famed garum business. The town was finally abandoned in the sixth century CE. Over the centuries the massive stones were used as foundations for other structures, so the area remained a well-known place to build a fishing village. As you will read in chapter 2, by Georgeos Díaz-Montexano, the area was still being mapped in using ancient maps. In light of the contemporary earthquake and possible smaller tsunami schedule of the area, it is quite likely that the sedimentation combined with smaller tsunamis and just kept building up the coastline and backing up the ever-shrinking rivers flowing in this direction. Thus, it became impossible to get any type of boat into the area by the sixth century, when it was abandoned. The fact that the British Museum has a map attributed to Ptolemy that locates a very large series of walls in the first century CE at the area where Cerro del Trigo is located today will be presented in Georgeos's chapter. The map of Ptolemy has the designation of this site as "Tartessos." The geophysical work we did was only to confirm that there was buried in the mud some of the ancient contours of the site, but it is nearly impossible to excavate this muddy environment down to thirteen meters. I do not think we have to, thanks to the Bonsor and Schulten excavations of the Cerro del Trigo site in the 1920s. They found the last remaining piece of what they knew was the last remaining wall of an ancient walled city in their excavations, but they did not know how to follow up with the work. The stones embedded in Cerro del Trigo are the same stone types that we encountered offshore during our work there in 2016. They could only have arrived at Cerro del Trigo with the ancient tsunamis and offshore earthquakes.

I return to the giants whose shoulders we stand upon in our Atlantis work in southern Spain. George (Jorge) Edward Bonsor Saint Martin, a French-born British archaeologist, historian, and painter, was the older of the two men. He was born in 1855 and spent time in Spain painting and later as an archaeologist. Renowned for his love of the ancient legacy of Spain and the preservation of archaeological sites, he discovered and studied numerous Spanish sites. Bonsor is credited with some of the most important discoveries of the late nineteenth and early twentieth centuries, including the necropolis and the amphitheater at Carmona and locations at the ancient Roman town of Baelo Claudia in Cádiz and the Setefilla area in Lora del Río. He died in 1930. Adolf Schulten, the younger of the two, was born in Elberfeld, Rhine Province in 1870 and lived to be ninety years old. Schulten received a doctorate in geology from the University of Bonn in 1892 and studied in Italy, Africa, and Greece with support from the Institute of Archaeology. Like many of this generation of archaeologists, he had a passion for developing the history of Europe as a whole, and archaeology was the means to this end. After obtaining the chair of ancient history at the University of Erlangen, he continued his work in Spain with great dedication, and to this day he is considered a key influence on archaeological study in Spain. He and Bonsor collaborated on their project in the Doña Ana Park in a specific location that they felt represented the best possible chance for excavation: the Cerro del Trigo southeastern marsh site. It became an obsession for Schulten, who, thirty years after the death of Bonsor, continued to write about the possibilities of discovering the original site of Tarshish/Atlantis in that marsh.

I feel like I "met" Bonsor twice during my work on Spain: once in the field in the Doña Ana Park at Cerro del Trigo and a second time when I went through an archive of his work in New York City. All science builds theories on the shoulders of the "giants" who came before us, who had inklings that there was something more that needed to be done, even when they themselves could not do it in their own time. Past generations had far fewer technological resources, but they had insights from the opportunity to look at a site before nature and human activity had changed it. They worked in far-flung places, and they did research in a world that was far simpler and technologically less sophisticated than our own but was able to inspire the awe of encountering the unexplored. My search for Atlantis and biblical Tarshish began in an archive at the Hispanic Society of America (HSA) in New York City on Broadway between 155th and 156th Streets on the edge of Harlem. The Hispanic Society was founded in 1904 by Archer Milton Huntington and is one of the gems of New York City that few people see. It is also a wellspring of information on archaeology in Spain. It has libraries, collections, and exhibitions, and it is where the archives of modern Spanish life and culture are found in the United States, including the archaeology of Spain. At the Hispanic Society of America, I was able to examine all of the original correspondence and writings of a twentieth-century giant of Spanish archaeology, George Bonsor, who had been the first to do a systematic excavation in Doña Ana, which in the end he declared to be the ancient city of Tarshish. Elected to the Hispanic Society of America in 1905, Bonsor was considered in Spain and all of Europe and in the Americas as one of the great archaeological figures of the nineteenth and early twentieth centuries.

Bonsor's correspondence and writings were archived at the Hispanic Society following his death in 1930. I looked at over a thousand pieces of the massive documentation of his work in Spain. I also looked at his original twentieth-century attempt to establish both Tarshish and the lost city of Atlantis, which he located in modern-day southern Spain. Bonsor had done excavations of some of the most important sites in Spain and had a very special interest in a site in the Doña Ana Park in the early 1920s. Despite catastrophic environmental events that had closed more and more sections of the ancient bay (which stretched from present-day Cadiz and Huelva in the south all the way to Seville in the north), Bonsor noted that small river boats could still reach Seville in the north through the first century CE. The great swamps and marshes of the Doña Ana Park in southern Spain were a silent reminder of what had been an active marine economy and perhaps one of the largest protected port sites in the ancient world. Bonsor spent many years charting the ancient routes and rivers of Spain and was very impressed by the Guadalquivir River, which continued to change direction and shape with great frequency through the Middle Ages, and which created the 250-square-miles of the Doña Ana Park. The effects of the shifting of tectonic plates and the massive tsunamis that accompanied the earthquakes in the region would only be fully understood years after Bonsor's work in the 1920s. But he already recognized that the changing river routes and settlement patterns of the region (from the ancient Mediterranean coast to the smaller Roman-period rivers that ran through Doña Ana Park) altered the course of history.

THE MYSTERY OF THE NAMES: ATLANTIS AND TARSHISH

I return to the mystery of the names Atlantis and Tarshish because I am not satisfied that they are not one and the same place in different configurations and in different time periods. Just as Atlantis disappeared mysteriously from the literary record, so too did Tarshish. As Tarshish was a port city at the end of the known world, so too was Atlantis. In much the same way that speculation ran about the lost port city of Atlantis, by the middle of the nineteenth century, ancient Tarshish had been placed by explorers and geographers in India, Spain, Crete, Cyprus, and off the coast of Lebanon and Turkey.

The search for Tarshish was often a surrogate research topic for the search for Atlantis. As the greatest archaeologist of ancient Spain, Bonsor was not immune to the allure of the topic. Tarshish was important to Bonsor because he was classically trained and he knew from the Bible and classical sources that it was a port city at the farthest end of the Mediterranean. He also knew that the area of southern Spain was known by two very distinctive designations: Tartessos and Al-Andalus. Classical sources such as Herodotus, Strabo, and Pliny's *Natural History*, as well as a late Roman source, Avienius's literary itinerary *Ora Maritima*, all mentioned Tartessos in southern Spain. *Ora Maritima* is an interesting and unusual source, since it is a poetic work that connects many of the pieces that none of the other ancient literatures (besides Plato) do. The poem *Ora Maritima* (Sea Coasts), written by Avienius in Latin in the fourth century CE, purports to be conveying information that goes back a thousand years earlier (perhaps to the time of Plato), and it traces the different parts of ancient coastlines and peoples that must have still been known in the fourth century CE. He writes about the ancient coast of Spain, and is especially conversant with the area at the Pillars of Hercules. He also is aware of the name of the island of Gadir (Cadiz),which he says was originally called Tartessos. Although it is hard to know if he is alluding to an earlier island in the area or not, he relates the area to the tenth labor of Hercules in Geryon and places it, as do other ancient sources, beyond the Pillars of Hercules. It is hard to know if Avienius was aware of these connections from sitting in a library or from actually visiting these places in antiquity. His knowledge of the specifics of the rivers that seem to be approximate to the rivers in the Doña Ana is one of the reasons why Adolf Schulten and George Bonsor took this literary source seriously in the 1920s.

By the fifth century BCE, Herodotus specifically placed Tartessos "beyond the Pillars of Hercules" (the same place that Plato's source had placed Atlantis) (*Histories* 4.152). The first century CE Roman historian, Velleius Paterculus, dates the founding of Tartessos to the twelfth or eleventh century BCE. In my research, the first questions I asked were whether Tartessos was predated by an even earlier island beyond the Pillars of Hercules, and whether the ancient name Tartessos preserves the biblical name of Tarshish. There are just too many coincidences here that tie Tartessos to the location that also fulfills most of the characteristics of Tarshish. Most scholars think that if there is a close linguistic link (which is their similar names) and there are some points of convergence of ancient sources, then the two places are connected. The second area I was most interested in during my research was where the city/

port of Tartessos/Tarshish was exactly located in the large southern coastline of Spain. There are those who contend that Tartessos/Tarshish was located at the modern city of Huelva, which does indeed have Bronze/Iron Age finds that could be consistent with a Phoenician port city. Some think Tartessos/Tarshish was located at ancient Cadiz (near Huelva). Bonsor's theory was that Cadiz and Huelva were ports in the period of Tarshish, but the original Tarshish (or Atlantis) was located inside of the vast expanses of the ancient Doña Ana marsh. Ancient Tarshish's location was something that grabbed Bonsor's professional attention as early as 1918. He wrote a whole project for Tarshish in an outline I found in his correspondence at the HSA dated to 1918. This included one of the most beautiful and carefully mapped areas for the ancient island-port of Tarshish that I have ever seen. He mentions in the second paragraph of his proposal that in September 1910, German professor Adolf Schulten's research in the area had motivated his own interest. His 1918 treatment argues for the need for Spanish researchers to do the work on a Spanish expedition. Letters from Schulten to Bonsor are in the HSA files and include one dated April 22, 1910, that was about the significance of the undertaking. In this same file, one particular envelope caught my attention. It was a rather large white envelope marked "very fragile." In it was a map that was from the original work of George Bonsor, dated August 25, 1921. On the map, he indicated where he thought the places to dig were for the ancient island-port of *Tarshish*.

I also found a single envelope that had ten of the most beautiful photographs of ancient Roman buildings, which Bonsor found in the area where he thought Tarshish was originally located. Why, I thought, did he take this small and humble fishing village to be the remains of the original port of Tarshish/Atlantis? The reason is that as you look at the photos you see that they were not of a small and humble fishing village. Rather, they show massive stones that were used as the foundations for the buildings that were built there. These stones could not have been brought from another location to this place but had to have been there for thousands of years. Much more important for me on my visit to the Cerro del Trigo site of Bonsor was the examination of the stone. The stones in Cerro del Trigo are quartzite and shale, and the bricks that are found there are late, but the quartzite and shale in the middle of the park is highly unusual. Later when we were doing our work off of the coast and examining the stones found on the shelf off of Chipiona and Rota Formation, we discovered that the debris there was also the same type of quartzite from Cerro del Trigo.

Beyond the photographs and the maps that Bonsor included in his work, he wrote about the significance of the discovery of a place such as Tarshish for the people and the culture of Spain. Archaeology, as much as it is a scientific discipline and directed by dispassionate investigators about artifacts, is also about people. Scholars who choose to excavate one site over another are making a conscious choice. As much as Bonsor was interested in the ancient Tartessan people and this site of Doña Ana, he was also interested in the national identity of the people of modern Spain as it relates to the discovery of Tarshish. As much as his investigations of ancient Spanish sites were about the ancient people of Spain, they were also about the dignity and identity of the modern nation. In writing my own book, *Digging through History*, one of the most important elements that I discovered is that as much as ancient historians are writing about the past, they are also writing about the present. By the beginning of the twentieth century, Spain's time as a major superpower had passed. Bonsor's work reflects his interest in establishing Spain as the site where civilization began. He writes to the president of the HSA, President Huntington, on February 21, 1920, about his recent (first) visit to "the supposed" site of Tarshish. He was taken to see a variety of items that were from the Roman period but the abundance of building materials in the marsh indicated to him that the "island" area at the tip of Doña Ana had indeed been inhabited in a period before the Romans. As he himself notes: "When

Professor Harry Jol in Italy examining the metal sample of "orichalcum" in 2015 with XRF. (Courtesy of Harry Jol, University of Wisconsin-Eau Claire)

we begin digging there [at these Roman places] we may find underneath like in the site of Troy, the ruins of an older town, Phoenician or Iberian." His enthusiasm for this project was enormous. He wrote of his encounter with the local leadership: "When those quaint aristocratic people . . . heard that I was pretending to discover a mysterious place in their property, where many thousands of years ago King Solomon had sent expeditions for materials to build and adorn his magnificent temple . . . their surprise was extraordinary!" It is clear that Bonsor saw this project as the great pinnacle to his extraordinary career in archaeology for and about Spain. For Bonsor, it was what put Spain at the center of a prehistoric European/Mediterranean culture that was more than just the Spanish history; it was at the center of an ancient culture that helped to formulate other cultures—including the Greeks.

TRACKING ORICHALCUM FROM ORIGINAL ATLANTIS AND THE REST OF THE ATLANTIS CIVILIZATION

> In the first place, they dug out of the earth whatever was to be found there, solid as well as fusile, and that which is now only a name and was then something more than a name, orichalcum, was dug out of the earth in many parts of the island, being more precious in those days than anything except gold and silver.
>
> —Plato, *Critias*, 114b

For some, the existence of orichalcum would prove the very existence of Atlantis. In 2015 when a shipwreck was found off the coast of Sicily with what seemed to be a significant cargo of thirty-nine ingots of the metal in its hold, some researchers immediately deemed it evidence of Atlantis. The problem was that the shipwreck was from only 2,600 years ago, putting it just a few generations before Plato wrote about it in the distant past. But for me, this was confirmation of another kind. For me, the discovery of the continued use of orichalcum in the Mediterranean Sea 2,600 years ago was a sign that the Atlantis civilization was alive and still functioning just generations before Plato wrote down his epic dialogues *Timaeus* and *Critias*. It was another clue that Atlantis may have had a new manifestation on different parts of the Mediterranean that continued to use an orichalcum-like substance right through the Roman period. It is found in a number of different manifestations in the writing of Herodotus, in coinage, in sacred vessels [no less than in the Solomon's Temple of Jerusalem] and in the writings of other Greco-Roman writers. What gave it significance was probably not the word itself but the association with the original Atlantis. It is an alloy that is ill-defined in many periods but is more precious than gold and silver because it had been famously decorating the original Atlantis walls of the fortress, the royal palace, and the Temple of Poseidon. Much of the evidence I collected between 2010 and 2020 was connected by other researchers to the location of Atlantis. Orichalcum, an alloy found in the Homeric period, was one that every reader would have seen as both unique and well known in Plato's time. The connection between orichalcum and Atlantis is crucial. Finding what it was and where it was originally mined led us back to southern Spain in 2010, but in 2015 it led me to make sure what the actual alloy was in the "orichalcum" of Sicily and to confirm the date of the shipwreck. Plato writes:

> And they covered with brass, as though with plaster, all the circumference of the wall which surrounded the outermost circle; and that of the inner one they coated with tin; and that which encompassed the acropolis itself with orichalcum which sparkled like fire. (*Critias*, 116b–c)
>
> All the exterior of the [Poseidon] temple they coated with silver, save only the pinnacles, and these they coated with gold. As to the interior, they made the roof all of ivory in appearance, variegated with gold and silver and orichalcum, and all the rest of the walls and pillars and floors they covered with orichalcum. (116e)

The abundance of this rare metal in use on so many pillars and floors and the fact that the mines are there is very significant. What is orichalcum? Orichalcum is first mentioned in the eighth or seventh century BCE by Hesiod, and in the Homeric hymn dedicated to Aphrodite, dated to the 630s BCE. Plato places it squarely as a significant piece of Atlantis architecture. The name orichalcum derives from the Greek *oros* (literally "mountain") and *chalkos* ("copper" or "bronze"), meaning, we think, "mountain copper" or "a place where copper is abundant in a mountain." Orichalcum has variously been held by scholars to be a gold/copper alloy, a copper-tin or copper-zinc brass, or a metal that is simply no longer known. However, in Virgil's *Aeneid* the breastplate of Turnus is described as "stiff with gold and white orichalcum." This means that it was known by his readers as a special metal by the time that Plato wrote about it and also after the time of Plato. For many researchers of Atlantis, as one site in one period, one of the most common quests in their research is to find the metal "orichalcum." Orichalcum is the mysterious metal that provided a unique sheen to the outside of the fortress, the royal palace, and the Temple of Poseidon of the original Atlantis according to Plato.

The reports of the orichalcum find were reported in newspapers and science journals worldwide. The thirty-nine ingots thought to be "orichalcum" were discovered in a sunken vessel (a thousand meters off the coast of Gela in southern Sicily on an ancient sea shelf only ten meters below the surface) and dated to the Iron Age (another forty-seven were found buried in the mud). We were working on the 2016 update on our earlier work in Spain in 2015 and one of the most important parts of the building materials of Atlantis according to Plato involved a series of different types of stones and a unique metal covering at the Temple of Poseidon: Orichalcum. When we were working on our proposal for our return in 2016 the stones and the covering seemed to be a culturally unique elements that could help locate the Atlantis civilization. The elements of orichalcum required metals that simply do not appear in every location, and thus its presence would have required the moving of elements from place to place to give the various Atlantises a comparable "look."

We were asked to assess the find firsthand. Sebastiano Tusa, Sicily's superintendent of the Sea Office, told us the thirty-nine ingots had been found by a team of divers who were exploring the shipwreck. Knowing that orichalcum was connected to the story of Atlantis, I wanted to see what exactly this find off Gela was made of and perhaps to be able to assess the provenance of the mined metals that were melted down to create the ingots. The provenance of heavy metals in metals and ceramics was something that our team had worked on in Rhodes on ceramics that were unprovenanced in the Rhodes seaport but which we tried to identify by analyzing the elements of pottery from pottery that was provenanced and comparing them. This was a near-impossible task in earlier periods. Today, with a pXRF (portable X-ray fluorescence) handheld device, we can tell a lot more about metals and pottery and eventually where they came from. The five elements that make up traditional recipes for orichalcum are: copper, zinc, tin, lead, and nickel. These elements are not found in every region, so if the Atlantis "look" had to be shipped in, it is likely that it started with an area where all five are found and can be shipped after they have been smelted. The Rio Tinto area by southern Spain is one of those locations, and although it is very difficult to say that it was the only place where it might have been shipped in from, it is important to know that the "recipe" may have started there and then become the "look" that added a sheen that was "Atlantean" even when the elements were coming from another region. According to Josephus Flavius, the first-century CE Jewish historian, the vessels in the Temple of Solomon were constructed from orichalcum. Not because the Jews were from Atlantis but because there was a tradition about orichalcum that considered it to be most rare into the first century CE. We could not directly account for the Sicily shipment as an ancient orichalcum being shipped from Spain to Sicily or from Sicily to another location but its existence testifies to the ongoing significance of elements from the "Atlantis" civilization being used into the Iron Age. We conducted our own analysis of the ingots using a pXRF machine on loan to us from our geoscience team that included Professor Harry Jol from the University of Wisconsin, Eau Claire. XRF is a new technology that with a handheld device can give an enormous amount of data. Energy Dispersive X-ray florescence (EDXRF) technology, like the one we employed is a fast, non-destructive way to analyze ancient samples. EDXRF works by irradiating a sample with non-destructive X-rays in order to facilitate inner orbital electron excitation within a target element. The replacement of the ejected electron results in the creation of a secondary (i.e., fluorescent) X-ray which is detected by sensors on the nitron fluorimeter. We then can tell by parts per million (ppm) what the sample was made out of by analyzing the elements in the sample without ever destroying the sample. This type of work has two big advantages. First, we can tell what the sample is made out of without having to break off a piece and subject it to a chemical analysis, which is both time-consuming and destructive, but it also has the advantage of allowing us to compare the same done with other samples of metal from specific places and often determine where the sample of metal was from. There are specific elements which we know orichalcum was historically made from, and often all of those metals are not found in the same place. That the metal was found aboard a ship that grounded near Sicily is only one part of the analysis. The metal was mined somewhere else and was being transported when it ran aground off Gela (and based upon the pottery and shipwreck remains is dated to the sixth century BCE). This implies that the metal would still have been in the conscious memory and vocabulary of the Greeks. The orichalcum that we analyzed from Sicily had all of the elements that are in fact found with similar ppm of the elements in southern Spain. The question I ask now is not what others asked. The original Atlantis was gone by the time this ship ran aground off Gela, but the orichalcum may have continued to be mined for years after the destruction of the site to supply the other Atlantises with the Atlantis "look." This would have been an artifact that connected many of the sites in the Western Mediterranean with the Eastern Mediterranean, where the original Atlantis had originally stood. Orichalcum was originally considered as being a stone—that is, an ore giving high-quality "mountain" copper. This is explicitly said in the first paragraphs of book 34 of the first-century *Natural History* of Pliny the Elder (he writes *aurichalcum*). According to the geologists I consulted, the only copper ore that has a gold-like color is chalcopyrite, $CuFeS2$. I am also very interested in what may seem like an unusual combination: the Hebrew name *Tarshish* is sometimes used in the Hebrew Bible in a sense of a stone and translated in the Septuagint and in Josephus's writings in Greek as chrysolite (another Greek formulation of "golden stone").[3] While orichalcum and chrysolite are not the same, they are similar and may indicate an attempt to locate a mineral source. This ore is the most common primary copper ore, and Pliny may have referred to a particular rich mine, consisting almost exclusively of the ore when he referred to it. He does not say where the mine was located, but mentions that the mine was exhausted by his own time.

The making of orichalcum required copper-tin or copper-zinc and other elements and even if all of the elements were available creating the alloy required a form of smelting that was quite advanced. The writings of a Pseudo-Aristotle in *De mirabilibus auscultationibus* describe orichalcum as a shining metal obtained during the smelting of copper with the addition of "calmia" (zinc oxide), a kind of earth formerly found on the shores of the Black Sea. This description may just be a later attempt at defining the alloy, but Spain has several polymetallic deposits located in the Iberian Pyrite Belt (IPB) that would have supplied the basic components. The IPB measures 60 km wide by 250 km long and extends from the southwestern coast of Portugal near Setubal to the Guadalquivir River near Seville, Spain, in close proximity to the Doña Ana Park. Its use began in the Middle East and the Balkans around 3000 BCE. Tin appears to be necessary part of the equation and is a relatively rare element in the Earth's surface, with about 2 ppm, compared to iron with 50,000 ppm, copper with 70 ppm, lead with 16 ppm, arsenic with 5 ppm, silver with 0.1 ppm, and gold with 0.005 ppm. Ancient sources of tin were rare, and the metal usually had to be traded over very long distances to meet demand in areas that lacked tin deposits. Known sources of tin exploited in ancient times include (among others): Spain, Portugal, Italy, and central and southern Africa. Part of our interest in the exact measurements of the orichalcum ingots discovered off of the coast of Sicily was to determine if they were from a source in Italy or perhaps Spain. If they were coming from Spain, it would mean that these other Atlantises may have continued using orichalcum on their own architecture some 2,600 years ago to duplicate not only the architecture but also the style of the decoration. In this period the materials were still extant in Spain (it was only exhausted in the Roman period), and this would connect these places with not only the architectural form but the design of the original Atlantis. The fact that this metal associated with the decoration of the Temple of Atlantis is being used in the region in the Iron Age may tell us just how long the Atlantis civilization elements continued. The fact that Plato goes out of his way to describe the use of the orichalcum as an item on regular artifacts and being mined at the Atlantis site puts the location in a very specific series of places, including southern Spain. What we were looking for were clues connecting the other sites in the Mediterranean with the southern Spain site, and orichalcum was that element.

HOW STONEHENGE HELPED US FIND ATLANTIS— BUT NOT IN THE WAY YOU THINK

Stonehenge is a model for many Atlanteologists because it was built in the Chalcolithic period in massive construction, in the middle of nowhere with materials not from there and it suffered some type of cataclysmic end that we cannot fully understand. The concentric massive wall construction also is suggestive of Atlantis. I have always been intrigued by Stonehenge. I have taken my students to Stonehenge multiple times to introduce them to the nature of how following the stones tells us everything we want to know about an ancient site. What intrigues me is mostly how the ancients hoisted these stones up on top of one another using ancient technology, but also where they got the stones from in the first place and how they got the stones to what looks like an isolated plain.

Most people know that Stonehenge was built in perhaps the same period as Atlantis and is a massive stone structure sitting as it appears today in the center of a lonely plain in the United Kingdom. The fact is that the area where it sits in Wiltshire, England, has dramatically changed over the past five thousand years. But little could be done to find out if there were more of these stones since it is a protected World Heritage Site and too sensitive for massive invasive archaeology. The archaeologists suspected there were more stones below and around Stonehenge in the open field nearby that were buried over time. In their studies they showed noninvasively (but conclusively) that there are more massive stones in the fields nearby. The research showed traces of up to sixty huge stones or pillars that formed part of a much larger "super-henge." The magnetic signature of the agricultural dirt on the top layers was inherently different from the materials below and their magnetic signatures were traceable.

At Stonehenge they did not know if there were any more stones when they started. At Doña Ana, thanks to Bonsor and Schulten's pioneering work in the 1920s, we knew exactly where to start. The work at Cerro del Trigo involved creating a grid that moved north and south of the starting point with GPS coordinates. What's more, we knew the source of the rock deposits at Cerro, while at Stonehenge it was not altogether clear where the massive stones had been brought from. The stone of Cerro resembles the stone of the Atlantic Ocean. The history of the tectonic events and the mega-tsunami background explained the movement of the stones. The Cerro site, like Stonehenge, is excellent for magnetometers because it does not have the buried cables, electrical poles, pipes, and other distractions that can disrupt the signals for the magnetometers in populated areas. The one most important factor for Cerro was the fact that there are no other massive stones in the area under the surface of the sand. They were not cut from local quarries. They had been brought there by extreme wave events. Before we went in January 2020, Dr. Claudio Lozano went and checked the Atlantic floor for the second time. In 2009 he did the first survey during our National Geographic work and the conditions were not very good for his work in September 2009. He could do only two dives and collected data for only those dives. In 2016 he had the benefit of a decade of research in the area and did a more intensive study in May 2016 and the conditions of the Atlantic were more favorable. The field of stone on the ocean floor showed intense seismic activity and among many other discoveries, it suggested that it was the origin of the massive stone structures embedded in the dunes and may even have elements from the ancient city walls that ended up in the ocean, again thanks to the power of the mega-tsunamis.[4]

WHAT BONSOR AND SCHULTEN KNEW: SEARCHING FOR THE BURIED WALLS OF ATLANTIS

Back in 2009 when we walked around the Doña Ana marsh with ERT, I was skeptical of what could be done even if we did find a wall under the mud. One of the first articles that my colleagues gave me to read was by an archaeological group that had done work on Cerro del Trigo. Cerro del Trigo stands on what is called the transgressive dune systems of the Doña Ana spit (Fig. 1.5). It is the oldest known settlement on the right of the Guadalquivir estuary. It is literally sandwiched in between two dunes and therefore it protected whatever was embedded in the area.

What do we know about Cerro del Trigo? Well, it is perhaps the best documented of all of the marsh. Cerro del Trigo was a fishing and salting-industry town from the second to the sixth century CE and archaeologists at the University of Huelva returned to the place where Bonsor and Schulten worked in the 1990s and worked exclusively on the Roman-period structures. The process of fishing and salting made shipping to and from the open sea increasingly difficult, which may well explain why the Cerro del Trigo settlement was abandoned in the sixth century CE. Given the sedimentation patterns and the ongoing possibilities of tectonic and tsunami events, Cerro del Trigo slowly became totally cut off from the rivers that led to the Atlantic. The cities in the local area like Doña Blanca and Jaen have remains that are as old, showing how the movement was clearly closing the center of the ancient bay. The reason for such an archaeological gap in the space between is, clearly, that pre-Roman and older formations in the Doñana barrier are several meters below the ground surface.

The Cerro del Trigo location in the Doña Ana marsh hemmed in between two dune sections. (Courtesy of Philip Reeder, Duquesne University)

The walls which Bonsor and Schulten found in the area were not from the Roman-period fishing and salting structures. They knew that these Roman-period structures were built upon earlier foundations. Who, according to Bonsor and Schulten, were these early builders of the walls that they found in the 1920s? Tartessans. The stone pieces did not arrive to their resting places in Cerro del Trigo easily. They are indeed massive and there is no quarrying area in the marsh. The massive walls of stone buried more than three meters below the surface should not be there unless they were brought there by tremendous tectonic forces. It suggests that the stone foundations were from a catastrophic earthquake and tsunami that moved these massive stones from the sea bed, which has exactly the same type stones off of the coast. What is really remarkable about Bonsor and Schulten was that they came to realize this in 1925. Bonsor and Schulten saw these remains as not only Tartessos but the antecedent of an even more ancient city, like Atlantis. The ancient Tartessos and Atlantis had both been destroyed by catastrophic earthquakes and tsunamis in different periods and the pieces that did not get swept out to sea were used in later periods to provide foundations for later constructions.

The problem of not being able to see the walls of Atlantis because they were buried by subsidence in thick mud will always be the ultimate hurdle of researchers of Atlantis. If you cannot show the walls, then you cannot truly demonstrate to the casual visitor that Doña Ana is truly the place. Even with all of the scientific evidence and data, you end with the same visual of a mud flat. In places like Malta, the Azores, and Sardinia, you can see ancient walls; just not ancient enough to fit the account of Plato. In 2010, I wanted to return and do one noninvasive study of one location in the Doña Ana, but I did not have the time. In 2016 I returned to look at the site again but without the equipment. The last mystery of Cerro del Trigo requires a complete magnetometer survey of the area to determine if there are more pieces of the ancient walls of the ancient city still embedded in the dunes.

WHY CERRO DEL TRIGO CONTAINS
THE LAST PIECES OF ATLANTIS

Cerro del Trigo is one of the highest points of the marsh and is sandwiched in between two massive ancient dunes. It is the only remaining excavation piece of Bonsor and Schulten that revealed that below the Roman fishing village was a massive foundation stone that is so different from the surrounding landscape that they knew that it had to have been brought in and shaped to form the wall-like rock that he found in the 1920s. Yes, a Roman fishing village was located in the same area of Cerro del Trigo, but the Roman fishing village was placed there because it was the only place where these rock features were assembled and they were all there because they had been deposited there in antiquity.

The work which we began in 2010 was continued in 2016, and I returned in 2020 to Cerro del Trigo because we now had new information. Georgeos Díaz-Montexano had uncovered an ancient map from the British Library (Burney MS 111) that while attributed to Ptolemy in the first century CE is a copy from the fourteenth and fifteenth century. This is most probably where Bonsor and Schulten's excavations took place because it is approximately the same distance from the coastline of the Cadiz Bay as the dunes of the coastline to Cerro del Trigo.

It is rare to have a map of an area that you are working on that purports to be from the first-century CE geographer Ptolemy. Ptolemy's map making is extraordinary for the period but it also provides information that goes back much further than the first century CE. To be working on a site and have a medieval/Roman period map in one hand and our equipment in the other gives you a new perspective on how long a site can hold it secrets. This is most probably the Roman-period fishing and salting center.

The Bonsor/Schulten excavated wall from Cerro del Trigo, with Simcha Jacobovici (2016). (Courtesy of Simchaa Jacobovici, Atlantis Rising)

The Burney 111 MS at the British Library. The map of the area of Cerro del Trigo is found in the triangular shaped area in the left-hand side of the map surrounded by water with the center piece spelling out the name Tartes[s]os in Greek. Close up of the Tartessos mini-island inland from the coast with Gadeira (Cadiz). (Courtesy of Georgeos Díaz-Montexano)

At Cerro del Trigo with Georgeos (center) with the map spread on one of the areas of the fishing and salting structures. Although this is a medieval rendering of the first century map it has walls visible in the center of the sedimented area. Where did these massive stones for these walls come from? The area where the fishing village was located at Cerro del Trigo is all sand dunes except for some areas that contain massive stones that obviously formed the foundations for the structures that Schulten and Bonsor found during their own excavations in the 1920s. (Courtesy of Georgeos Díaz-Montexano)

There is something more that the Ptolemy map shows. Most scholars say that there is only one ancient version of the Atlantis story that is circulating in antiquity. In fact, there is a first-century CE version that is circulating in Alexandria, and Ptolemy may be the connection. Ptolemy was in Alexandria, and the Jewish philosopher, Philo of Alexandria, also mentions Atlantis in his "On the Eternity of the World" (26.141). The map gives us details of what the marsh looked like two thousand years ago and it appears to still have walls surrounding an area inside what would be called today: "Cerro del Trigo." The finding has been one of the most important contributions made by Georgeos for the research on ancient Atlantis in the Doñana Park and especially in the Cerro del Trigo area. Bonsor and Schulten associated the ancient foundation with the ancient city of Tartessos and Atlantis.

PROVING THAT THE ATLANTIS CIVILIZATION BEGAN IN SPAIN

One of the biggest problems in Atlantis research is that researchers are looking for one single site as if it is a "singularity" of existence that does not require a whole network in the area to function. If Atlantis was a great civilization like Athens, it would have to have adjacent service cities and villages nearby. Most or nearly all Atlantis searches start and end with a single site. Atlantis needs a whole chain of cities and adjacent sites to make it "Atlantis." If I look at Tenochtitlan, an island city of the Aztecs in Mexico, I have to know that there are a series of other villages and cities in the region that service and support the Aztec way of life and the mother city. Some searches for Atlantis locate it in an isolated site and never attempt to create the entire picture of what the period in this location was like. But if this is an island/port/ city, it needed to have a whole network of agriculture. To have archaeological evidence of a site, you need to be able to have groupings of "service" or sister cities that made a site like an Atlantis function. In order to have an Atlantis in southern Spain you have to have a nearby site like Jaen.

WHY ANCIENT SUPPORT CITIES MATTER: JAEN HELPS PROVE THAT THE ORIGINAL ATLANTIS WAS IN SOUTHERN SPAIN

The nearby Chalcolithic stone city of Jaen's design, artifacts, and time period set in the third millennium BCE is just this type of city, and its location in close proximity to roads leading to the Doña Ana port would make it an ideal site as a sister city. It is difficult to divide the topic of archaeology of the original Atlantis from the later site which will be known by another name: Tartessos. In order to establish the archaeological trail, we have to start with what we call the sister-city of Atlantis or better the "service" city of Atlantis, which we have at Jaen. There is no doubt that Jaen's Marroquíes Bajos site is from the third millennium when an "Atlantis" in the ancient bay of Cadiz would have been standing. The fact that there are artifacts from the early Bronze Age in the Jaen area that have the concentric circles on a jar from there and from the greater Seville area tells us that the symbol had meaning in the Bronze Age. It is not just an invention of the Iron Age memories of the artists at Cancho Roano and in central Spain. It is an ancient meaningful symbol of decoration that was not a shield, but rather a real place that like other concentric, nested, walled cities like Jaen was associated with a construction plan of purpose. The contribution of Georgeos's work to trying to rescue the site even as it is being constructed for new housing in the city is found in his article below.

WHAT IS THE ARCHAEOLOGY OF ATLANTIS?

In 2011, after the airing of the National Geographic documentary *Finding Atlantis,* I gave many interviews to reporters. I gave an interview to journalist, Mark Adams on the background of the work that we did in the south of Spain. As I explained to Mark, we did not go out searching for Atlantis. Our team accepts invitations to do our work in places where traditional archaeology is either not possible or is inconvenient. Usually this means a preliminary investigation on-site with some work being done and usually a return to finish the geoscience in areas we felt deserved further study. In 2012 I went to China to look at the remains of a medieval synagogue with remains under a hospital in north-central China for a possible project and in the same calendar year we excavated an ancient Byzantine church under a modern church in Nazareth. Most of the projects that my geoscience team go to examine are for the purposes of research. Our purpose is to solve problems and move the discipline of archaeology to be more noninvasive than invasive in its approach. When I tell my students that the geophysicists are doing pro bono work and that none of us are paid to do the research they often question me about "why we do it." We do not receive funding from film companies and most of our projects are local collaborations. We spend most of the year vetting proposals with the team of researchers and then raising funds from foundations to pay our costs. Our work has now been chronicled in twenty different documentaries and hundreds of conference presentations and publications, and it is based upon the premise that traditional archaeology is destructive, labor intensive, expensive, and largely ineffective and needs to change. Our group includes geoscientists, geophysicists, geographers, geologists, and allied sciences, and we always bring students to the field to teach our methodology. All of our staff and students publish in their own disciplines. We provide all of our research to the local researchers at no cost and offer our services when in country to other archaeological expeditions all to hopefully convince our colleague that geo-archaeology is effective, inexpensive, and not labor intensive and that it insures that in the future, when newer and better technologies are available there will be something for them to research at a site. Our group maps, defines, and often recommends where "pin-point" archaeology might be done for the local archaeologists to follow up on. To date our group has done sixty sites worldwide in six countries. When Mark Adams came to visit I was working other projects in Israel and looking at proposals in two other countries. At the end of the chapter where Mark presented his discussions with me in his book, *Meet Me in Atlantis* (New York: Dutton, 2015), he writes: "We shook hands and I watched him drive off. Only then did something occur to me: If Freund had made the most important archaeological discovery in history, why wasn't he going back to Spain anytime soon?"

The simple answer to this question is because our invitation was for one preliminary geoscience project to see if there is enough to justify a larger project. More important, each project, even a preliminary project, requires a scientific sponsor to ensure that if we do uncover a major find, we have a possibility of preserving the evidence with on-site help for a future follow-up project. To mount an expedition often takes years of planning, and it is always at the invitation of a local scientific initiative. We give our maps and recommendations, and it is the responsibility of the locals to follow up in the ways that they see fit. In fact, it was a colleague in Lithuania where I was working in 2016 on another noninvasive project associated with the Holocaust who pointed out the book to me. At the time, my group had been invited to see if we could help identify mass burials and destroyed synagogues in Lithuania. For most of the researchers in Lithuania it is nearly impossible to research using traditional archaeology. We can map, define, and recommend where to excavate and where not to excavate. The work was documented in a *NOVA* science series episode titled "Holocaust Escape Tunnel." It was named as one of 2016's top-ten science stories by the *New York Times*. It was essentially the same type of work that we had done in southern Spain. Instead of an legendary buried city in a marsh, we looked for a legendary escape tunnel out of a Holocaust-era burial pit built by hand under fifteen feet or more of mass burials and barbed wire in 1944. When students ask me what archaeological discovery I consider to be the most important one I have made in the past twenty-five years I always say: "the next one." What I now consider archaeological artifacts is quite different from what we were looking at even a decade ago. In the case of Atlantis, we were brought back to use our noninvasive techniques to look at a variety of new evidence that was part of a broader research focus.

THE ATLANTIS CIVILIZATION IN SOUTHERN SPAIN

It certainly does help to have an artifact like a memorial stone that resembles the site to make a case for confirming a site location, like this, which was found in Jaen; it mimics the site of Jaen and corresponds to the original design set out by Plato. When you read chapter 2, by Georgeos, you will see his own analysis, which parallels the stones of Badajoz in my original chapter on Atlantis. This is clearly not a shield or any other design, and the fact that a similar jar fragment was found near Seville makes it an excellent piece of archaeological evidence of the Atlantis civilization in Spain. Archaeologically, the other sixty thousand Chalcolithic artifacts discovered in the ancient Jaen city would be the kinds of artifacts that we would like to see for a city like Atlantis in the period of the early Bronze Age of the Chalcolithic period.

WHY MOTILLA DEL AZUER HELPS PROVE THE EXISTENCE OF ATLANTIS

Evidence of Chalcolithic and Neolithic sites are not the most visited or researched in Spain. The tomes written about the history of Spain center on the Greco-Roman period and then on the rise of Christian Spain. But Spain has some of the most ancient sites in Europe. There are decorated caves and cities that go back tens of thousands of years. It is from this vantage point that one

The Ancient Circular and Nested Walled City of Motilla. (Courtesy of Richard A. Freund)

has to view the "Atlantis in Spain" hypothesis. Most researchers that I corresponded with had one site, and when I asked them about the "service cities" necessary to provide logistical help to the ancient city they called "Atlantis" they generally had not considered the question The ancient "nested, concentric stone walls" of the site of Motilla del Azuer, in central Spain, is another piece of the puzzle. Motilla is from the Chalcolithic period and is another part of the "Atlantis in Southern Spain" service cities. It is located approximately one hundred miles from Jaen, and it is along the central trade routes that would have been a piece of the trade of the Chalcolithic period in Spain. Motilla is another enormous concentric circle construction around a major well for the area and is significant not by itself but as part of a network of ancient villages that would have stood in the same time period as Atlantis. As I studied the nested and concentric stone walls of Motilla [that had been reconstructed] I realized just how massive the construction was and how difficult it would be to totally destroy the evidence of its existence. The walls were what gave the site its distinctive look and what led archaeologists to fully excavate the site. Unlike Jaen, which was located in an area where construction of houses continued to this day, this village was a piece of a network in an isolated area where Greco-Roman, medieval, and modern building had not yet begun. It also constitutes what we were looking for in the Doña Ana. The remains of massive stone walls that could not be totally destroyed even by a mega-tsunami.

KNOWING WHAT HAPPENED TO THE SURVIVORS OF ATLANTIS IN SPAIN IS CRUCIAL

In order to understand an archaeological site's life, we must know its beginning, its middle, and its end; and more important, we must recognize that there are always going to be survivors of any destruction. The Atlantis civilization that I am writing about is tied to a place in southern Spain and its beginning is tied to the cataclysmic tsunami that formed the first ancient islands of Atlantis in what is today the mudflats of Doña Ana. For this to be accurate, we need supply cities nearby such as Jaen. But to understand what happened, you need to have a whole series of follow-up or successor cities that allow the events to have had some type of continuation. The existence of the Tartessan culture to the north of Doña Ana at places like La Mata and Cancho Roano allow the story of Atlantis to be carried on by survivors. The fact that these cities disappear in Spain after the Greek invasion may provide the key to the survival of the Atlantis myth among Athenians. It also requires one more step of research.

The second piece of archaeological evidence is the entire complex of villages in the central area of Spain, such as La Mata, Cancho Roano, and the other villages that we call "ritual or memorial" villages that were built as miniature Atlantises in central Spain in the Iron Age. No, they are not from the original period of Atlantis. They are, however, the results of descendants of the earlier city who felt they wanted to memorialize the ancient city with a site that probably provided them with pilgrimage opportunities and was indeed a miniature Atlantis, down to the metalworking expertise. Many civilizations built miniature versions of their holy cities that they congregated in to remember where they come from. The Jews, for example, began to construct miniature version of the Temple of Jerusalem after the Temple was destroyed by the Romans in 70 CE. They had elements similar to the Temple of Jerusalem meant as a place of meeting. These are standing stones with the symbol of meeting and remembering. The architectural features mimicked the Temple's structures but always in a smaller more stylized way.

The Cancho Roano interior concentric circles' walls, its holy of holies, its entrance, the stele that sat at the front of the entrance, the water trench that was dug to surround it, and the artifacts found at the site all bear witness in an ancient context to the archaeological remembered Atlantis. For this reason, it counts as archaeological evidence of the Atlantis story, albeit from descendants' memories or oral histories.

A third piece of archaeological evidence is the multiple cave drawings and ancient mapping attempts by ancients that have been discovered in the area from Badajoz to the area near Gibraltar. These pieces of evidence are important and now with modern imaging we have a better idea of just how accurate these maps and illustrations were.

HOW AND WHAT WE COLLECT AS EVIDENCE FOR THE EXISTENCE OF ATLANTIS IN SOUTHERN SPAIN: WHY MULTISPECTRAL IMAGING MATTERS AS ARCHAEOLOGICAL DOCUMENTATION

Photography and the illustration of objects are essential parts of archaeology. We document the site, artifacts, and the general location of a site with maps and digital photography that was state of the art some twenty years ago and has now been replaced by specialized processes like multispectral photography that reveals new details of ancient artifacts. This is an enormous leap forward in researching the archaeological finds of places all over the world where we have well-established sites that now have new ways to see the same artifacts. In our case, we are championing another noninvasive technique in the research of Atlantis since multispectral photography is noninvasive and the small details it reveals in a well-known object may indeed change the way we understand the object.

What constitutes a text? Illustrations on many surfaces from pottery to stone, metal to glass, and of course our beloved paper, papyri, and parchments. Multispectral imaging is a technique to recover and preserve damaged or illegible texts. Main, auxiliary, and transmissive lights produce a controlled spectrum of light, which our specialized camera then records. The bands of light range from the short reflective bands of UV through the visible spectra and into the long wave bands of infra-red. The different bands of light, particularly when combined in later processing, produces an image of the material that the naked eye cannot see. As part of the Lazarus Project, these scientists and others continue to perform groundbreaking research at top libraries and institutions around the world, including Cambridge, the Beinecke Library, the New York Public Library, the National Library of Wales, and many more. This topic may seem like it is not as important as the actual site visits and excavations of large landscapes in southern Spain, but in many ways it is an example how small details combine to create an Atlantis portrait.

The idea of looking at a map that has been produced by an ancient artist on a tapestry or a stone wall or cave may seem odd. It is not. Like the Old Stone Age cave drawings and stone illustrations found in the north of Spain, it is clear these artists were following a very ancient tradition in Spain and France of documenting their lives and their interests. It is perhaps the first documentation of history. The caves on the northern Iberian coast and slightly inland are just some of the many examples of ancient Paleolithic groups who lived in or by the caves and who illustrated their ancient world and lives. They felt a need to document and remember the animals, landscapes, people, and places that they knew, perhaps because they were on the move and would be able to remember where they were with this visual image, but it is also possible that they did these illustrations to remember a significant event or document a memory that had great meaning to them. In the beginning of the twentieth century, scholars debated how these ancients could have done such realistic drawings. Before C14 dating they argued that the drawings might be attempts by modern or medieval artists to record their own times or imagine the past that was long gone. Most of the scholarly arguments stemmed from a preconceived notion about the nature of Neanderthals and Old Stone Age peoples that they were incapable of this "higher" level of thinking and lacked the skills to do this type of work. One of the earliest drawings, an outline of the fingers of a very human hand from forty thousand years ago was at least possible. But the main body of the cave drawings from thirty-five to fifteen thousand years ago (dating of the illustrations and the artifacts remains a question but at least this is the current range of the dating) depict animals and landscapes.

Drawings of horses, bison, deer, and their surroundings are quite realistic; scaled to match the size of legs and heads; and included details like eyes, flesh tones, manes, ears, horns, tails, and expressions. The human figures are often to scale with hands and legs, their hunting gear very realistically placed. They even included motion and the conditions of an area where they hunted. Many of these illustrations sparked a lot of controversy because it was assumed that ancient people could not possess the intellectual and artistic abilities that made them possible. This argument has been largely resolved in the second half of the twentieth century with the new dating techniques, and it is clear that humans had the ability to imagine and create realistic images of natural settings, animals, vegetation, and people well before our conception of the artistic tradition of Europe took shape. The polychrome drawings are inspiring and aesthetically very appealing. They document animals that would be extinct by the time the Chalcolithic and Early Bronze Age began. The tradition of publicly showing the richness of their environment anticipates the illustrations that would keep the memory of Atlantis alive for the people in the south.

OUR IMAGING LAB IN BARBATE, SPAIN

I end my part of this chapter as sort of an introduction to a variety of ancient sites and pieces of evidence in southern Spain that are a part of Georgeos's research on "Atlantis in Spain." Most of what Georgeos has researched is found in Spanish-language articles that are not well known. I have been in contact with him since we started our reassessment to share with our team the fruits of his labors and to give him the opportunity to explain the evidence. In addition, the opportunity to bring new researchers into the conversation helped focus how we will be doing our future work in noninvasive archaeology. This is a translation of much of his work in which I attempt to capture some of the most important aspects that do not appear in my own writing.

At every one of the archaeological sites that I have worked at for the past thirty years we had a single designated photographer who, perched on a ladder, took stills of the site as it was in the beginning of the day and often again at the end of the day. The photographer sometimes had to develop film in a makeshift dark room in a basement or bomb shelter, allowing us to see the images for the next day's work, or we sent them off to a photo lab that allowed us to see better-quality images in a few days. Today, of course, this is all different. In an office in the hotel where we stayed in Barbate, Spain, one of the new techniques of noninvasive archaeology allowed us to assess information every night. In 2016, the researchers created a small imaging laboratory where we all could see the thousands of images that had been stitched together from the specialized cameras of the Lazarus Project, which were brought in to help "raise" new images from the old stones that absorb the original color in different ways. Dr. Greg Heyward of the University of Rochester and Ken Boydston, a computer specialist from Santa Barbara, showed us the results of their multispectral imaging sub-project at the stone walls near Badajoz and the cave illustration that overlooks Gibraltar. They added crucial details that show us just how much these ancients knew about what had happened in their own backyards. They also add to the body of information that we have on ancient events and this is one of the pieces of the future of Atlantis archaeology: Imaging and reimaging well-known pieces of evidence for more information. Most of the best imaging can be found in the film *Atlantis Rising* (2016), whereas Georgeos and I present only stills that capture a single frame of a very large illustration on a cave wall.

New Technologies for Ancient Images. (Courtesy of Richard A. Freund)

The sites are on the two extremes of what was known later as the "Tart-essan" cultural band that cut across central Spain and Portugal in Badajoz to the Straits of Gibraltar in the southeast corner of Iberia in the Iron Age over five thousand years ago. The organic materials used to create the colors provide us with the means to date these illustrations, but their details bear the travails of humidity and thousands of years of exposure. One of the only ways to bring out details is to see them with multispectral imaging that exposes them to light that uncovers elements no longer visible to the naked eye. The images give us a whole new set of data to assess. It shows, I think, that there were "spectators," "survivors," and lead to the evidence that is embedded in the landscapes and stone work around southern Spain. That is why the work of my Spanish colleague, Georgeos, brought us back to Spain in 2016 to look for the rest of the story.

Searching for Atlantis in 2016

Georgeos Díaz-Montexano

By the end of 2009, Professor Richard Freund was in contact with me to incorporate my research, hypothesis, and findings about historical-scientific Atlantology with the work he had done in Doña Ana. He introduced me to Simcha Jacobovici to make an updated documentary with my work ([*Atlantis Rising*] which was ultimately produced by James Cameron for National Geographic in 2016).

RESEARCH ON ATLANTIS

It is not the purpose of this chapter to detail chronologically the whole gratifying adventure with National Geographic and the filming team and producers, but to introduce the reader to episodes of my research and a more complete or extended analysis concerning the spots that have been filmed for the documentary and are linked to my hypothesis about Atlantis.

The symbol of the concentric circular metropolis of Atlantis, according to Plato's description of Solon and the Egyptian priests, on a ceramic pot from the end of the Bronze Age and beginning of the Iron Age (Tartessic or Turdetan) was found in the city of Jaen, Andalusia (Figure 2.1). Above, on the right, reconstruction of the metropolis of Atlantis, according to what was described in the *Critias*. Below, in the middle, sketch of the metropolis of Atlantis, as it appears in most books and encyclopedias. Underneath, reconstruction of the Chalcolithic city excavated by archaeologists at Marroquíes Bajos, Jaen (Andalusia).

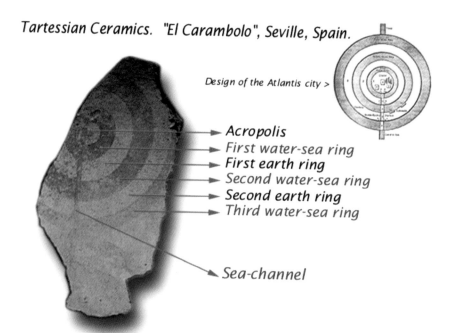

Tartessian Ceramics. "El Carambolo", Seville, Spain.

Design of the Atlantis city >

→ Acropolis
→ First water-sea ring
→ First earth ring
→ Second water-sea ring
→ Second earth ring
→ Third water-sea ring

↘ Sea-channel

Ceramic pot shard with map of an Atlantis city explained: a concentric circular macropolis with channels. (Courtesy of Georgeos Díaz-Montexano)

The Jaen circular walled city, the neighbor of Doña Ana, with ancient walls and moats. (Courtesy of Georgeos Díaz-Montexano)

It is common sense (as it is also explained in the *Timaeus* and *Critias* by Plato) that, if Atlantis really existed (as an advanced civilization or culture), its cities, towns, villages, and hamlets would have been built in its surrounding area: Andalusia and Portugal on the north and east, especially in the areas closest to the Atlantic coasts, such as Cadiz and Huelva, and most likely some places in neighboring Morocco, the nearest region to Atlantis island-city on the eastern side. These cities, villages, and hamlets would probably look like the main pattern of the metropolis, described as having several circular moats that were filled with water, alternating with rings of land or inter-moat spaces, encircling a small island where the acropolis or main area would be, along with the housing, temples, and more socially relevant buildings. This urban pattern was discovered at Marroquíes Bajos, a district to the north of Jaen. I was the first person to realize that there is a connection with the urban pattern of the concentric circular metropolis of Atlantis. I found it there first, at the beginning of this century, but sometime after I found the same pattern in other ancient cities of the Chalcolithic and Bronze Age in Andalusia and the Algarve, among other places within the Iberian Peninsula.

The existence of this concentric city inside a geographical area next to the place where Plato located Atlantis island—according to the notes his fifth-generation grandfather Solon brought from Egypt, if the Atlantis island really existed, it shows that the Egyptian priests could be inspired by any legendary ancient city in Andalusia from the Copper Age or the Bronze Age, as most probably the concentric pattern of cities and sanctuaries was a typical referent of many peoples from the Copper and Bronze Ages, who most probably would have made their first urban settlements by the end of the Neolithic period.

Do we have to accept as "mere coincidences" that in the places nearest to the site identified as Atlantis (according to the exact location given by ancient sources), there are in the Iberian Peninsula and Morocco, thousands of cave art depictions and ceramic pots that show the symbol or pattern used to depict the Atlantis metropolis? Is this just a "sui generis" design or motive, which has concentric circles and connects the central point to the exterior of the rings or circles, or is it connected with the city that had these characteristics? Is it merely incidental that the only place where there are macro-villages, big towns, or cities (according to the qualifying parameter I used) with this same urban concentric ring design (alternating moats or circular channels flooded with water with rings of land or inter-moat spaces surrounding concentrically a small circular island), is in these places near Atlantis? I don't believe so, and there are many thousands of people who agree with me. They don't believe all this is a set of "coincidences," as most historians and archeologists typically assert to pretend that such evidence does not exist, disregarding circumstantial proof and arguments so reasonably convincing as these, and many other arguments I have been submitting and publishing for more than twenty years.

The unexpected historical milestones of "Marroquíes Bajos," Jaen are:

1. The oldest and largest city (macropolis) in Europe.
2. The oldest fortified macropolis (walled with bastions) in Europe.
3. The oldest fortified macropolis with hydraulic engineering in the world.
4. The oldest macropolis in the world that had paved streets and bridges to cross over flooded moats and canals, thousands of years earlier than in classical civilizations.
5. The only ancient fortified macropolis in the world with hydraulic engineering of an Atlantean design—that is, built with a concentric circular urban pattern that, as in the capital of Atlantis, alternates water-flooded trenches with earth rings, around a central island (acropolis).

Despite all these historical milestones and regardless of the public complaint that Simcha Jacobovici made to the world—in the documentary *Atlantis Rising* by James Cameron—about how builders had taken over the few remains that survive after most of the archaeological site was buried (with the consent of politicians) by private and public buildings, the acting government has announced it will give the green light to projects to build above these spaces (despite being fully protected by the heritage law), even above the area that preserves the only bastion of the more than one hundred that are estimated to have constituted its huge fortified walls. That is to say, the little that is left of this ancient site, where a proper and correct value could be realized through reconstructions and interpretation for tourist exploitation, will be buried forever under buildings (where supposedly they can be seen underneath crystals) thus losing any real possibility of being able to visit them and study them in situ.

The Scientific Atlantology International Society (SAIS) with the support of the Instituto Almenara for the progress and development of Andalucía, the authors of this chapter, and the producers and researchers for the documentary *Atlantis Rising*, produced by James Cameron et al., have begun a campaign on Change.org for "Marroquíes Bajos" to be declared a Historical and Archaeological Heritage of Humanity, and thus stop its definitive destruction. The builders and politicians who support builders for economic interests continue acting as if nothing and no one can stop them from completely destroying the little that remains of an archaeological site that is very important for Spain and for all humanity. For this reason I invite the readers of this book to join the campaign.

Nearly a thousand years before the Egyptians and Sumerians did it, there was an evolved maritime civilization already using big rowing and sailing boats in Southern Andalusia. Ancient Egyptians credited the goddess Isis with the invention of sailing. Legend has it that Isis thought about erecting a post with a piece of linen to capture the wind so as to speed up the ship on which she was traveling when she was looking for her son Horus. However, the Greeks state that there were two inventors: either Daedalus, when he escaped from the Minotaur labyrinth in Crete, or the god of the winds himself, Aeolus. Nowadays, however, we can say that sailing was not invented by Egyptians or Greeks, but by the ancient inhabitants of the Atlantic-Mediterranean coasts of the Iberian Peninsula. They were the first to build ships powered by sails and oars, as evidenced by the fact that the most ancient depictions of sailing vessels to date are found only in South Iberia. The most recent scientific radiocarbon dating points to more than six thousand years ago, which is at least a thousand or five hundred years before the most ancient cave paintings of an Egyptian sailing vessel, and more than two thousand years before the first ships built by Mycenaean and Minoan Greeks. This finding, now known for several decades, was discovered at the park of Alcornocales de Jimena de la Frontera, Cadiz, in a cave known as Laja Alta.

I have been defending the hypothesis that these ships and this port scene are testimony to, at least, the existence of a high civilization or great sea culture, a West Atlantic or Atlantean-Mediterranean civilization, previous to Phoenician and Tartessic times, that proliferated not very far from the Strait of Gibraltar (Pillars of Hercules), and that such a culture could be no other than the culture described by the Egyptian priests to Solon, who decided to call it Atlantis.

A passage of the *Critias* by Plato can be recognized in the harbor scene of the cave Laja Alta (see Fig. 2.3), where Atlantis's international port is described the following way: "The sea-way and the largest harbor were filled with *ships* and merchants *coming from all quarters*, which by reason of their multitude caused clamor and tumult of every description and an unceasing din night and day" (Plato, *Critias*, 117e).

The 2016 National Geographic documentary—following my hypothesis—succeeded in filming a quarry area and a possible port, submerged eighteen meters deep three miles southwest of the coasts of Chiclana de la Frontera. Several large stone anchors were photographed and filmed (among other structures), close to each other (almost in a row), and have an archaic style that seems to point to the Chalcolithic period. The depth and

The Ancient Cave drawings near the Coastline Cave of Laja Alta, Jimena de la Frontera, Cádiz. (Courtesy of Georgeos Díaz-Montexano)

distance from the coast as well as the dating coincides with the ships depicted at Jimena de la Frontera from around six thousand years ago, so the anchors might well belong to the same kind of Atlantean-Mediterranean ships, which could belong to the same civilization or great sea culture of Atlantis.

As I mentioned in the beginning of the chapter, everything related to the filming of all the possible underwater evidence that might give support to my proposed theory about Atlantis (which is shown in the documentary as hardly an advancement) is contained in another book currently being edited. That book will be focused on matters of underwater archeological, seismic, and geological evidence, and the results will be developed in the next documentary of the same series about the historical-scientific Atlantis, produced by James Cameron, under the direction of Simcha Jacobovici. However, I will discuss superficially a short selection of some of the evidence here, with the exact location of the archeological sites not divulged for obvious security reasons and for the protection of cultural heritage. I hope the reader will understand that I wanted to present as much as possible without going beyond areas that we were able to do. I present some of the evidence in images that were available.

SOME UNDERWATER SITES AND ARTIFACTS

The following is excerpted from many of my articles. See the bibliography.

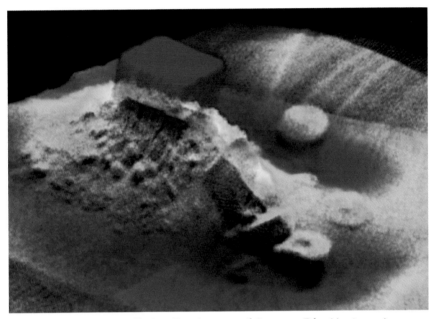

Sonar image of the area off of Cadiz. (Courtesy of Georgeos Díaz-Montexano)

Figure 2.4 Location: Area close to the Gulf of Cadiz, between Iberia and Morocco.

Description: Column drums (it appears officially recorded this way in the submarine archeological sites register). The place is described as a group of cylindrical column drums. Some possible megalithic blocks can also be seen.

Dating: If these possible column drums did not fall from a ship during the period of Phoenician and Tartessian colonization or in Roman times, and they are really in their natural site ("in situ"), then they might be dated back to 7,500 years ago as the most recent possible date, according to their depth. Hardly a thousand years later, the sea level had risen and the remains were completely covered by water.

Grinding stone underwater found near the Cadiz site. (Courtesy of Georgeos Díaz-Montexano)

Figure 2.5 Location: Area close to the Gulf of Cadiz, between Iberia and Morocco. In the middle of the Gulf of Cadiz in the southern part of San Fernando de Cádiz.

Description: Possible menhirs or megaliths and slabs or ashlars drilled through their center with a vertical or Tau-shaped slot, discovered by Miguel Aragon by the late 1990s. More recently, following this author's hypothesis, a possible ancient seaport has been discovered with possible breakwaters, quarries, and several kinds of stone anchors that could be traced back to Chalcolithic and Bronze Age times.

Dating: If these possible lithic artifacts in the shape of ashlars, slabs, or blocks, carved as bricks, monoliths etcetera did not simply fall from a ship in Chalcolithic or Bronze Age times (and normally they would not be carried thousands of miles on a ship for building purposes) and they really are in their natural site, then they could be dated back to 6,500 years ago as the most recent possible date, according to the depth they are at. Therefore, if they were artifacts from ruined buildings in situ, like the possible seaport and the quarries found at the same site, this archeological evidence should be dated (as the most recent date) between 7,200 and 6,200 years old, these dates being the last time the area was above water. Hardly a thousand years later, the remains would be covered by the sea.

Multiple pieces of columns, building blocks and slabs. (Courtesy of Georgeos Díaz-Montexano)

Figure 2.6 Location: Area close to the Gulf of Cadiz between Iberia and Morocco, to the south of Barbate.

Description: Remains of a temple or unspecified building, completely wrecked, with rectangular blocks chaotically dispersed and some sections of the walls with its course blocks still visible. It shows a solid appearance, with signs of destruction by earthquakes and tsunamis.

Dating: It is unquestionably a very ancient construction that was probably built before sea-level rise above its current level if we consider the shallowness of the remains of this building, and that it is in the middle of a great plain or flat surface with sandy bottom where there is hardly any natural rocky outcrop, offshore right in the Gulf of Cadiz. The best Paleo-oceanographic Atlantic studies have proved that the last time the average sea level was just below the place where these ruins are was 10,000 or 9,600 years ago. This building definitely could not be attributed to the Phoenicians or the Romans, and neither could they be attributed to Tartessus reign that was no more than 3,000 thousand years ago. It is difficult to relate them to any known Chalcolithic or Neolithic culture from any part of the Occident. Whatever culture or sea civilization built this construction, they had reached a level of architectural evolution that was not known again until several thousand years later.

Note: These building ruins could only be reasonably linked to Atlantis, as described and located in primary written sources, as they start exactly in this same area in the Gulf of Cadiz. We could be before the ruins of the kingdom of Gadeirus, the second son of Poseidon and Cleito. The kingdom of Gadeira—it is said—was named after him, which was at the north end of Atlantis Island, next to the Pillars of Hercules, right in front of the current Gadeira or Cadiz, such as it is stated in *Critias* 114 a–b. Gadeirus is the only name Solon kept as testimony to the indigenous language of Atlantis's inhabitants. Solon translated the indigenous name *Gadeiros*, following its meaning and equivalence (as it is said in *Critias* 1113e) as *Eumelos*: "the good sheep and/or goats stockman" or "the one who has many sheep, goats, or small livestock." About the other indigenous names in the story, Solon only conveyed them translated into Greek, guided by its original meaning. For years I compared the name *Gadeirus* and its feminine derivative *Gadeira* with all the languages known and studied in the world. I consulted all the existing databases and lexicons, but I only found its perfect match in the family of Semitic languages from Asia Minor and the Near East such as Ugaritic, Syrian, Aramaic, and Hebrew. The voices Gad, Gade, and Gadi only exist in Semitic languages, with the same meaning of "goat" and "sheep," and the term *GDRh* as "Sheepfold for small livestock, goats, and sheep." With this etymological research and this discovery—which I explain in great detail in another of my books—I could prove that the indigenous language of the island inhabitants translated by Solon as "Atlantis Nêsos" (the island of Schu's descendants, that is, the equivalent to Atlas) was a Semitic language. Thus, it is common sense to deduce that the Atlantis civilization could have been the "mother or grandmother" civilization of all Mediterranean civilizations and cultures and Semitic countries because the language families appear so similar.

The massive artifacts found off of the coast of Cadiz. (Courtesy of Georgeos Díaz-Montexano)

Figure 2.7 Location: Area close to the Gulf of Cadiz, between Iberia and Morocco.

Description: Possible column drums with circular column shafts or huge grindstone disks located south of Isla Paloma, Tarifa; they are arranged around a great stone bulk in at least two groups, and one possible third group. The group of possible column drums consists of three big stone drums, two of them almost vertical, one of them buried by almost half, and the third one reclining between the other two. The other clear group of great stone drums or huge grindstones is very close, and it is composed of several drums almost horizontally, one on top of the other, as usually happens when dealing with razed drum columns, such as is seen in archaic Greek temples when columns have fallen down either by earthquakes or because they have been intentionally torn down.

Dating: If these possible column drums did not fall from a ship and they really are in their natural setting, in situ, according to their depth, they could go back at least 10,500 years, the last time this area existed as dry ground. Only a thousand years later, sea level would cover them.

Note: There could be at least two drums, but it is possible there are three. The most common viewpoint is that they are simply "grindstones," but it is difficult to explain how those "grindstones" would have been taken from a Phoenician or Roman quarry (which would be quite far from the current coastline) and how they could have rolled after falling until they came together in two groups, following more or less a line or a pile, as it is usually seen in any collapsed column. It is also difficult to explain how they could have fallen "by chance" right on top of each other, fitting horizontally into place, in accordance with their inferior relief or curvature (within their concave and convex areas) almost like a puzzle. It is equally bizarre to assume that they might have fallen from a ship that was transporting them and they ended up placed this curious way at that depth. In addition, most of them are too wide or too tall—as regards the thickness of the edge—to be simple "grindstones"; hence, they seem more like column drums with an average diameter of one meter (approximately) or one meter and a half. At any rate, even if they really were huge "grindstones," it would be more sensible to think that their original location was where they are now—that is, that they were in situ, as part of some quarry where these sort of devices were made, or maybe because they were part of a grinding factory, in which case it would likely be a settlement that could be dated between 10,600 and 10,000 years old (according to its depth), at the very least, because only one thousand years later it was covered by the sea, as sea level had risen up to five meters.

The evidence of bell-shaped capitals, similar to archaic Doric capitals, gives force to my hypothesis that proposes that they are not grindstones.

They have all the earmarks of capitals similar to Doric style, which also showed the same system of cylindrical drums to make the shaft of the columns. Doric capitals are usually bell-shaped or trumpet-shaped, and these samples found in the deep sea in front of the Strait of Gibraltar are also shaped this way, although they seem higher than those used by Greeks and Egyptians. Obviously, they would not be Greek Doric capitals, as there has never been a Greek temple around the area, and Phoenicians did not use that order, but rather the Ionic order, mixed with other Egyptianized and Orientalized styles. It could be said that these Atlantic capitals, although similar to Doric capitals, show a more archaic or primitive appearance, which would be more consistent with an older civilization, as it was, actually, with the Atlantis civilization.

For more information, read my book: *Tartessos. Hallando Su Metrópolis: Un mapa griego bizantino de origen clásico ofrece el punto exacto de su localización* Atlantología Histórico-Científica no. 3 (CreateSpace, 2012).

The Burney MS 111 from the British Library map of the Tartessos site made in the medieval period. On the left, Miguel Galindo del Pozo, Vice President of the Scientific Atlantology. (Courtesy of Georgeos Díaz-Montexano)

· 3 ·

The Dead Sea Scrolls Again

$\mathcal{B}$iblical scholar William Albright characterized the discovery of the Dead Sea Scrolls as the "greatest archaeological find of the 20th century."[1] We usually refer to the Dead Sea Scrolls (DSS for short) in two ways. One DSS collection is the one centered at Qumran in what was eleven caves that circled the village. These number over a thousand documents. The other DSS collection contains the hundreds of items that have been discovered in caves along the Dead Sea from differing parts of antiquity and also represents a literary treasure chest in fifty miles of caves along the Dead Sea. The Qumran Dead Sea Scrolls are disparate works: copies of the Bible; biblical commentaries; and legal, historical, and theological texts from the third century BCE or thereabouts to approximately the first century CE when it is assumed the Qumran was destroyed. The people who put the texts in the caves around Qumran may be different groups, but it is clear that they saw the village as a way of demarcating the hiding places for future generations. Many different types of texts and objects were hidden in the fifty miles of caves along the Dead Sea, and they were produced by many different hands. The use of the caves is the connecting piece. Having worked at Qumran and at the largest of the other caves, the Cave of Letters, my perspective on the Dead Sea Scrolls is different. I would say that the Dead Sea discoveries represent the greatest concentration of archaeological finds for the origins of post-biblical Judaism and Christianity in both the twentieth and twenty-first centuries. Although there was a sense that everything had been discovered by the 1960s, it is clear that with the new technologies and techniques more texts and objects will continue to be discovered.

Before the discovery of the Dead Sea Scrolls, most people thought that all of the ancient Jews shared a single narrative of Judaism, a shared veneration of Jerusalem and its leadership, and shared theological constructs that were documented in the Hebrew Bible and rabbinic Judaism. Before the discovery of the Dead Sea Scrolls some scholars thought that perhaps the Hebrew Bible itself was of a much later origin and not at all an ancient text. It is rare that a discovery changes the way we think about the world. That is why every discovery is a big discovery.

After the discovery of the Dead Sea Scrolls, we learned that there were competing Judaisms in antiquity, and that the Hebrew Bible and rabbinic texts only show a version of the whole picture. The Dead Sea Scrolls required scholars to reassess what they thought they knew about the period and to start viewing the same events with a different background narrative. In short, new discoveries may change the way we view existing evidence. Of course, that is the nature of scientific inquiry.

In 2019, I held a "Rediscovering the Dead Sea Scrolls" Symposium at Christopher Newport University in Virginia, where I now teach, and attempted to create a framework for future work around the Dead Sea. The list of presenters included Dr. Adolfo Roitman of the Shrine of the Book, in Jerusalem; Dr. J. Randall Price of Liberty University, who was a part of the 2017 excavations at Cave 12; Dr. Archie Wright of Regent University, whose topic was "Social Media and Qumran," and Dr. Michael Daise of the College of William and Mary, who spoke on the "Second Temple Literature and the Dead Sea Scrolls." I lectured on the "The Other Revolution at Qumran: Geoscience and Archaeology in the Dead Sea Caves and the Future of the Dead Sea Scrolls." I reviewed the types of subsurface mapping technologies that we have been using for twenty-five years, and suggested that these should be used in every single cave that had already been visited during "Operation Scroll," and in other excavations. Until recently, the finds had been almost right below the surface, despite the fact that the vast majority of these caves contain centuries of roof fall on the main cave floor. The recent work in 2017 was prompted by possible new looting of caves by Bedouin, and even more recently in 2020 and 2021 the situation in and around the caves was complicated by geological forces that are consuming the road system, while political upheaval required a much more robust Palestinian and Israeli coordination than it did when we worked twenty years ago. In 2019 we assumed that there would be future excavations, and that they would include more advanced equipment, not just traditional digging. Within a year, even during Covid-plagued times, several discoveries were made both near Qumran and near the Cave of Letters in Nahal Hever. Interest in less accessible caves has yielded more Dead Sea Scroll materials as well.

In 1999–2001 we worked at the Cave of Letters, but we investigated the possibility of working at the Cave of Horror, which sits just across the

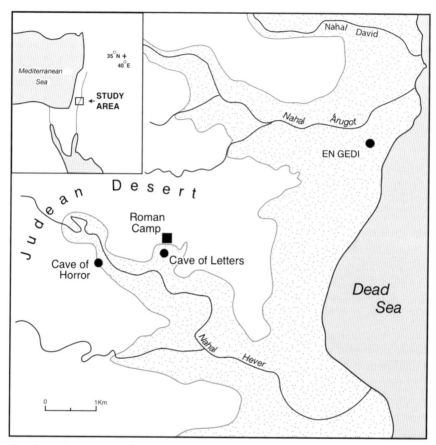

The Cave of Horror and the Cave of Letters on the Dead Sea map. (Courtesy of Philip Reeder, Duquesne University)

stream. In our excavations at the Cave of Letters in the year 2000, we were given the ability to return to the Cave of Horror, but chose not to attempt to transfer all of our equipment because of the difficult access, which would require an extremely expensive climbing infrastructure. The other reason why we did not follow up in the Cave of Horror was because of the original reports from Yohanan Aharoni, which indicated that the major finds were mostly the remains of the dead (hence the name "Cave of Horror"), and because it was relatively small cave for a team of ten with equipment to work in. We were working simultaneously at the Cave of Letters and at Qumran in 2001, and our aim was to use the equipment that we had to explore the massive Jewish cemetery at Qumran noninvasively. The Cave of Horror, also known as Nahal Hever Cave 8, was another Bar Kokhba–era rebel cave, which was given its name when the remains of forty men, women, and children were found inside. It is also located 260 feet below the cliff top of the Dead Sea Nahal Hever area that was originally explored in the 1950s by Yohanan Aharoni and again in the 1960s by Aharoni and Yigael Yadin. The identification of burials and the possibility of being involved in the recovery of Jewish remains was not part of our planned excavations, and further deterred us from working the cave in 2000. In the sixty years since Aharoni's and Yadin's excavations,[2] the attitude toward the treatment and excavation of human, especially Jewish burials had dramatically changed, becoming a far less usual practice to disturb the final resting places of human remains.[3] Aharoni also found Chalcolithic pottery fragments, small shards with what appear to be burial inscriptions, small pieces of what he could see was elegantly written Greek that he identified as one of the minor prophets' biblical texts in the Cave of Horror. He also discovered more coins in this small space than were discovered by Yadin in the much larger Cave of Letters. It took a recent visual identification of possible looters in the cave to encourage the Israel Antiquities Authority to mount a 2021 excavation that revealed some of the most significant finds from the Chalcolithic period, and translation of biblical fragments of Zechariah and Nachum[4] that confirmed Aharoni's work from the 1960s. For studying Jewish resistance, perhaps the most important ethnic markers are the caves, hideaways, and escape tunnels. Archaeologists have found more than 450 ancient cave systems in all parts of Israel, including many that were dug into mountainsides. These cave systems and hideaways were elaborate constructions with fake walls, shafts, and secret openings that the Jews used to launch guerrilla-style attacks and hide from their attackers. There is more to discover in these caves, and advancing technology will help reveal the secrets.

AFTER THE HOLOCAUST
THE DEAD SEA SCROLLS ARE A REBIRTH

Could it be that the Dead Sea Scrolls, so amazingly exhumed from their long forgotten cave-burials and suddenly transported over the space of some twenty centuries to the attention of the world, were hailed unconsciously by myriads as a symbol of luminescent hope in an age of otherwise unrelieved darkness?"

—Rabbi Dr. Nelson Glueck,
President of Hebrew Union College

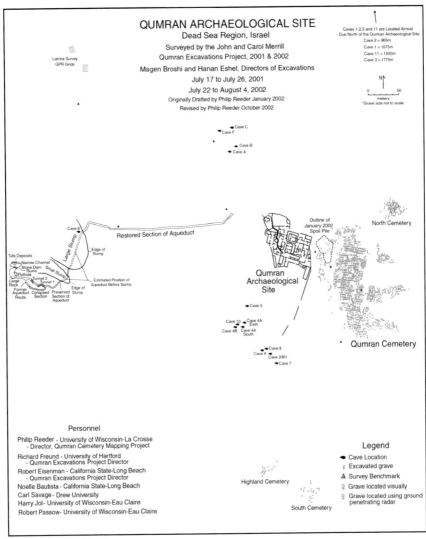

Mapping of the Qumran Excavations Project. (Courtesy of Philip Reeder, The Qumran Project)

Can one archaeological discovery really change history? I could name six or seven different archaeological discoveries that have changed history, but I chose to focus on the Dead Sea Scrolls because unlike other discoveries that changed the way we view the ancient world, the discovery of the Dead Sea Scrolls changed our understanding of ancient *and* modern religious history. More than any other archaeological discovery of the past century or more, the

Dead Sea Scrolls stand as an example of how a discovery has caused historians to go back to the proverbial "drawing board" and reconsider the ideas or pre-conceptions that they had about Judaism, the origins of Christianity, and the Bible. Many of my students think that all of the mysteries of the Dead Sea Scrolls have been solved since they are now available to scholars all over the world online. In fact, the importance of the Dead Sea Scrolls will continue for the future as scholars puzzle over the meaning and the influence of the ideas in the Scrolls. Like Plato's writings on Atlantis, the Dead Sea Scrolls are connected with many different places. One place, Qumran, and the caves nearby on the Dead Sea, is considered the place where the Scrolls were written. But it is not altogether clear that Qumran was the only place these Scrolls came from. In addition, the Dead Sea Scrolls and other manuscript discoveries from around the Dead Sea and Judean desert are themselves a part of a larger mystery of why this desert region seems to have served as a repository of so much almost unparalleled ancient religious thought. In our own work at the University of Hartford's projects in the Judean desert from 1998 to 2002 at caves along the Dead Sea and at the site of Qumran, a village near the eleven caves where the Scrolls were discovered, I became aware about how significant these discoveries are not only for ancient history, but also for modern religion. The original mystery of the content of the Dead Sea Scrolls has, for the most part, given way to a second mystery: What do the Scrolls mean, and how have they influenced modern religion? Part of our research included a search for other caves and to see if there is much more to the story. This is a thoroughly modern search using the high-tech equipment that we used in our search for Atlantis. Many of the maps that we developed have GPS locations for future study, and I am certain that as the political situation on the West Bank improves, many new archaeological expeditions will follow. This is why archaeological research is part of historical research, as researchers try to unravel the original ancient context of the written material.

I was suddenly struck during our work at Qumran and the caves by how the methodology of archaeology concerning the Scrolls has changed over the years. Everyone admits that the Scrolls were for the most part not discovered by organized and scientific excavations. In fact, the provenance of the Scrolls will always be a question because they were largely found and brought to scholars from local Bedouins, who rarely shared the exact location of their discoveries. We puzzled for almost a decade over the Scrolls, which were eventually assigned to the Cave of Letters from other caves nearby. Once the large number of unique Psalms Scrolls, fragments of the Pentateuch, are reassigned to the Cave of Letters, the cave suddenly took on a totally different "religious" meaning that it lacked when Yigael Yadin excavated it in 1960–1961. Today we still marvel over the discovery of the letters of Bar Kokhba in the Cave of Letters, but we also marvel over the religious authorities who produced the scores of Psalms manuscripts that were taken from the cave in the 1950s (and assigned to a nearby non-Israeli cave) only to be reconstituted and reassigned to the Cave of Letters thanks to excellent scholarship. The context of the discovery matters, and at Qumran it is not only the context but assumptions about the Dead Sea Scrolls in the eleven caves that continue to influence our understanding of the Scrolls. Sometimes a technique helps redefine the archaeology. Our method of using electrical resistivity tomography (ERT) and ground penetrating radar (GPR) at Qumran and in the caves has redefined the way that ancient caves can be investigated. The fact that almost all of the discoveries in the caves were found on the top layer of all of the roof debris in the entrances to the caves suggests that our work may just be beginning. To end it now would be tantamount to an archaeologist just excavating the top layer of an archaeological mound and never attempting to see if there are other layers. Our work has confirmed that we need to have a new generation of research on the caves. The thousand or more caves along the Dead Sea that were quickly investigated by many different projects need another look with the GPR/ERT approach to see if they contain buried materials like those found in the Cave of Letters, which might usher in a totally new era of Dead Sea research.

Sometimes method and the public telling of the story of the Scrolls do help define and sharpen what we know about the Scrolls. An example is the new "Shrine of Book" at the Israel Museum in Jerusalem, which displays some of the Scrolls. The Israeli curator, Dr. Adolfo Roitman, has redefined the way the Scrolls are displayed, and by doing this he has also redefined the way that the Scrolls are understood by the museum-going public.

We started out work at Qumran in the mid-1990s when the "old" Shrine of the Book was still telling a story that had been defined from the 1950s and the early 1960s. It was an interesting story of a little-known sect of Jews living on the Dead Sea primarily before the rise of early Christianity. The archaeology of Qumran revealed that there was indeed a massive defensive feature. They had multiple water installations, a sophisticated system of capturing the water, a large area to eat, a pottery shop, no apparent living quarters, a cemetery containing men and women in more than twelve hundred in-ground burials, a strange structure in the midst of the cemetery with a single burial within and an unknown relationship between the various Scrolls in the nearby caves. There is still no absolute consensus about who the Qumranites were or if the Scrolls were even written there. If we judge the water installations by later rabbinic interpretation, they are not really easily categorized as rabbinically Jewish. The burials tell us little about the ethnicity of the individuals buried there, and the comparisons with the mysterious sect of the Essenes continues to vex scholars. Yet, beyond doubt, the discovery of the Scrolls and the village of Qumran captured the imagination of the world in the 1950s and 1960s in a way that no other archaeological discovery has done. But the meaning of the Scrolls became after 1965 a part of the national narrative of the modern State of Israel and were enshrined in their own iconic "Shrine of the Book" as a part of the new pantheon of the Jewish state. Even with no Temple and no priesthood, the Dead Sea Scrolls and their home at the Israel Museum in Jerusalem became the new Temple of the modern religion of Israel and the curator became the equivalent of the modern high priest of this secularized society.

We began working with the "new" curator of the Scrolls in 1996 when the Scrolls were being displayed in the "old" Shrine of the Book in the mid-1990s and we continued to work with him as our own work at Qumran progressed. We made a short documentary of the young curator, Dr. Adolfo Roitman, in 1997 (titled *The Shrine and the Scrolls*), which featured him scrambling around Qumran trying to tell the story that he had been taught by his predecessor about the relationship between the Scrolls and the caves that were located in close proximity to the village of Qumran. Over a decade later, Dr. Roitman has built a new conception of the Scrolls and has chosen to display them at the Shrine of the Book in Jerusalem in a totally different context—and to tell a different story. Today it is a story of the ancient manuscripts of the Bible and the group (or groups) that preserved these traditions, and it is about the modern State of Israel. Our short documentary was the first video that involved the new curator and the legacy of the Scrolls and the Shrine that housed them. The Shrine of the Book had become famous in Israel and the world as the modern day "Holy of Holies" of Israel. I use the video today in class to show how change in archaeological work changes the message of the same buildings, artifacts, and texts in the blink of an eye. I realize how different the new story of the Scrolls is from the old story of the Scrolls, and how this tells us a lot about how history works.

Our work at Qumran was similar to the new Shrine's progress. Just as the Shrine was embracing its role as a "mausoleum" to house the ancient Scrolls, it also became a way to help the Israeli and non-Israeli public understand the ancient story and the modern import of the Scrolls. It was a parallel series of changes in the archaeology and the display and the understanding of the Scrolls that prompted me to see the importance of the Scrolls today. Most people think that because biblical archaeology deals primarily with the ancient period, our understanding of the history is static. In fact, it is in flux. Every single discovery can change the way we understand an ancient site or discovery and in the case of the Scrolls our work has changed the way cave work can be done. It became clear just how fluid this changing history can be when I saw one of our famous discoveries cited in a book on geophysics and archaeology in 2006. In the last figure and last words of *Handbook of Geophysics and Archaeology*, by Alan J. Witten the author writes about how new technology has revolutionized the study of archaeology and uses our work at Qumran as an example. He ends his book: "While this feature is likely a cave, it remains to be determined if this cave contains any information dating to the period of the Dead Sea Scrolls."[5]

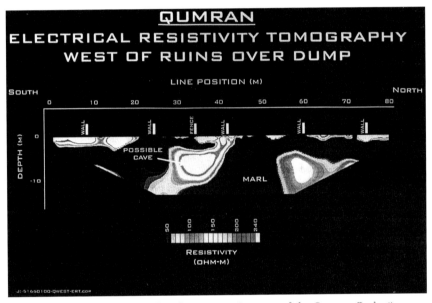

Electrical Resistivity Tomography of Qumran. (Courtesy of the Qumran Project)

The figure is used there to demonstrate how new technology allows us to go back and reinvestigate sites for more information. In this book, part of why the Dead Sea Scrolls is an excellent example for understanding the influence of religion and archaeology in the writing of history is that while new methods and techniques in excavation may actually force us to rewrite the history of a location, that history is influenced by a whole series of layers of history writing as well.

HOW POTTERY, FRUIT PITS, AND NAILS CHANGED OUR UNDERSTANDING OF THE DEAD SEA SCROLLS

I want to give one small example of how an archaeological discovery has changed our understanding of the Scrolls. In our 2001–2002 excavations at Qumran, we discovered some collapsed caves. We discovered a collapsed cave, for example, in one of the most inaccessible cliffs of the village but in close proximity to the other caves that also ringed the Qumran cliff face. Using ERT and GPR scans we discovered the cave, and went in. Instead of Scrolls we found some mats, ancient pottery, and ancient fruit and olive pits. While we were excited to find the collapsed cave, we were at first puzzled by the signs of human activity inside of a cave. One of the great mysteries of Qumran and the Dead Sea Scrolls has always been, where did the people who wrote the Scrolls live? There are no living quarters inside of the ruins, and this fueled speculation that the Scrolls were placed there by Jerusalemites and not by the Essenes. The Essenes are a mysterious and ascetic group mentioned in the writings of the first-century CE historian Josephus Flavius (and others). They were one of a number of "sects" of the Greco-Roman period (Pharisees, Sadducees, and Zealots are others, for example). The Essenes resided on the shores of the Dead Sea and were supposed (by most) to have been the authors/scribes who wrote and deposited (most if not all of) the Scrolls in the caves around this village.

Despite these ancient accounts about the Essenes, the odd missing pieces of the archaeological record at Qumran allowed people to say that it was not inhabited by a large group like the Essenes, but rather it was a winter palace (the Dead Sea is warm even when it could be snowing up the road in Jerusalem) for some official and the settlement has nothing at all to do with the writing of the Scrolls. It has always been speculated that the group lived in makeshift tents like other desert dwellers and so there is simply no evidence of their domiciles. But it is unsettling to archaeologists to base an argument on the lack of evidence, so the debate continued. So the discovery of human activity in a cave may signal something of great importance that may affect our understanding of the Scrolls. The human activity in a cave indicates to us that some caves may have been for living and some for storing Scrolls. In fact, about six years earlier, Hanan Eshel and Magen Broshi, the archaeologists we worked with during our 2001–2002 project, had discovered using a metal detector a mysterious trail of tiny ancient nails that led toward the caves. These nails, which may have held together sandals that were worn by some of the inhabitants in the Roman period, show that the residents trekked out to the caves regularly. The debate over how many people lived at Qumran and whether these are the people who wrote the Scrolls is still open. A new form of pottery analysis has aided this debate. Today, thanks to two new technologies, we know that the chemical signature of some of the pottery jars in which the Scrolls were found is in fact the same pottery that came from the Qumran site. So it appears that at least some of the Scrolls and some of the people of Qumran lived, worked, and were involved in the placement of these Scrolls in the caves where at least some of them lived (either for short periods, during the hot days, or permanently). While the arguments about the archaeological finds that surround the Scrolls continue (the original excavations from the 1950s were never completely published), the Scrolls themselves have changed the way we look at ancient history and modern religious history.

WHY ANCIENT WRITING CONTINUES TO INSPIRE US IN THE MODERN PERIOD

Our knowledge of the ancient world is so limited and fragile. We have ancient texts from excavations in India and China that no one can read and understand. Because of a series of fortunate events, we have been able to unravel the library of discoveries from ancient Egypt and Mesopotamia, and so have something to compare to the Bible. The Bible is a very limited knowledge base. It is made up of just a fraction of the stories and accounts that were circulating in antiquity. Perhaps one of the most controversial issues of archaeology and literary studies today concerns when Hebrew began to be written as a distinct language. It is controversial because many of the traditions of the Hebrew Bible point to very ancient events—for example, the creation of the world, the ancient flood, the Patriarchs and the Matriarchs, the sojourn in Egypt—which all occurred way before the ancient Israelites had their own written language. In what language were these original stories communicated? When did the ancient Bible scribes write down these traditions for the first time? Who were the sources of this information? How much leeway did a scribe have as he wrote down the word of God?

Although people realize that oral traditions have been maintained by many religious groups for thousands of years, the process is very mysterious. Who were these faithful people who served as "human books" of memorized information? In Islam and Judaism to this day, memorized and recited materials are maintained together with printed and read materials. People who can memorize large portions of holy texts are venerated in Buddhism, Hinduism, Islam, and Judaism, and Jews still refer to the Talmud by the ancient designation of "Oral Law," despite the fact that it has been written down for fifteen hundred years. The earliest Hebrew writing (which may have been a creative adaptation of the Egyptian hieroglyphs or pictographs) did not emerge as a full-fledged and distinctive language until the ancient Israelites were already settled in the Land of Israel and coalesced as people sometime in the tenth century. The discoveries in archaeology over the past 150 years taught us this.

The systematic archaeological excavations over the past century of have turned up only a handful of written pieces from the historical Land of Israel that allow us to date the development of Hebrew in the eleventh or into the tenth century BCE. This seems to coincide with what we know from the history of the Bible and the development of the ancient Israelites. In the period of the United Monarchy of ancient Israel (which was the period of King David, in the tenth century BCE), Hebrew emerged as one of the examples of this unique, united people whom we refer to as the Israelites. Even though the first seven books of the Bible refer to events that took place before the tenth century BCE, the archaeological evidence points to the fact that these traditions only began to be written down in the unique Semitic dialect of Hebrew in the eleventh and into the tenth century BCE.

Like a child maturing to the point of being able to ask "where did I come from?" so, too, Jews, Christians, and even Muslims may find in these unique written accounts preserved in the Scrolls a way to understand how their foundational doctrines are all rooted in these same texts. These are the oldest Middle Eastern manuscript versions of the biblical-esque apocalyptic scenarios shared by Jews, Christians, and Muslims. These are the some of the oldest manuscripts that trace basic ideas of initiation, anointing, covenant, rules of the order, cosmic war, sexual conduct, leadership, succession, and a host of other themes that later became standard parts of rabbinic Judaism, Christianity, and Islam. Because these documents can be dated before the rise of these faiths, we can view these Scrolls as the tangible launching pad for them in a way that is different than just the Hebrew Bible. Writing was an amazing, unusual activity in the ancient Near East, so the discovery of something as large and diverse as the almost one thousand Scrolls manuscripts is really unparalleled. Most writings that have been discovered through systematic archaeology from the ancient past usually have consisted of tomb and symbolic artistic presentations, record keeping, receipts, religious registers for internal purposes, correspondence between high officials or religious figures, or purely theological documents to ensure that the leaders of the cult knew what they needed to know. Even the great accounts of Mesopotamia and Egypt that were preserved are so fragmentary that even when they are pieced together, they do not give us a coherent system of religious ideas. Having ancient narratives put together in a running national epic was a revolutionary idea in antiquity. We appreciate Homer's labor in the *Iliad* and the *Odyssey* precisely because it was a unique endeavor. The Egyptian *Book of the*

Dead, which continued to develop for over a thousand years, is an example of how ancient writing was not a single author's work but the work of many hands. By the tenth century BCE, some of the earliest parts of the narrative were being written down even as a new historical period had begun. By the ninth and eighth centuries BCE, Hebrew writing had developed in earnest. Unfortunately, there are no manuscripts of any sustained size from this period, just short graffiti, a few inscribed pieces of Hebrew writing on stones, steles, clay tablets, bones, amulets, signets, shards, and bullae. Even though the material culture does not tell a coherent narrative, it shows us that writing was important. From the ancient Bronze and Iron Ages, few papyri and parchments survive. The only place where manuscripts might survive would be in a hot, dry, constant climate with perhaps a salt deposit or two to preserve the materials' organic matter. The Dead Sea was that place. Israel has a few different and unique microclimate zones that has preserved its history in ways that simply are unique. The fact that Jerusalem, the capital of the ancient kingdom of the Israelites and later the Judeans, was located close to this depository of the caves of the Dead Sea is also important. Located on one of the great land-bridges of antiquity from Africa to Asia, the Dead Sea Transform was the "Fort Knox" for ancient travelers from the Rift Valley of Africa to the depths of Asia. Travelers moving north and south and then east and west for tens of thousands of years followed the Syrian-African Rift, a tectonic plate on the earth's surface that passes by the caves along the Dead Sea. The caves provided a convenient hiding place for the material culture of different peoples. On the Dead Sea, there are nearly fifty miles of limestone caves that are situated adjacent to the lowest point on earth. These natural limestone caves were created tens of thousands of years ago as the ancient Lake Lisan receded and left the Dead Sea and the Sea of Galilee dislocated from one another with the river Jordan connecting them.

The Dead Sea has a unique environmental footprint on the earth's surface; it is only there that these caves could exist, and it is only in these caves that manuscripts such as the Dead Sea Scrolls could have been preserved for thousands of years. What strikes people first and foremost about the story of the Scrolls is that in precisely the place where we would need to have ancient documents preserved (ancient Israel), there is a natural environment (the Dead Sea caves) for the protection of ancient documents. After many years of speaking to people who have followed the story of the Dead Sea Scrolls more than any other archaeological story (save Atlantis), I have found that they see in the story of the discovery of the Scrolls more than just a discovery of a cache of ancient documents, they see them as a type of "message in a bottle"

Mapping Ancient and Modern Israel. (Courtesy of Philip Reeder,
Duquesne University)

YIGAEL YADIN: THE SCROLLS, THE STATE, AND THE HAND OF GOD

The timing of the discovery and the creation of the modern State of Israel is perceived by many as more than just a coincidence. Many religious people refer to it using religious terminology such as "miraculous" or even "the Hand of God." Many secular archaeologists are uncomfortable with this type of terminology, but they realize that it is one of the reasons why Qumran and the Dead Sea Scrolls at the Shrine of the Book at Jerusalem's Israel Museum are one of the most visited sites for religious pilgrims. Yigael Yadin, in his book *The Message of the Scrolls* (1957), relates a version of the "unseen" Hand of God argument, not only because of the fortuitous timing of the discovery, but the implications for the nascent State of Israel: "I cannot avoid the feeling that there is something symbolic in the discovery of the scrolls and their acquisition at the moment of the creation of the State of Israel. It is as if the manuscripts had been waiting in caves for the two thousand years, ever since the destruction of Israel's independence, until the people of Israel had returned to their home and regained their freedom."[6]

The "Hand of God" argument works in many unseen and unfathomable ways. The discovery of the Scrolls in the caves along the Dead Sea could have taken place in the Middle Ages, or during the eighteenth and nineteenth centuries when French and British archaeologists and Bible scholars scoured the landscape of Israel for new discoveries. The Bedouin (a nomadic Arab group living mostly in desert areas), who roamed this part of the Near East in the 1920s or 1930s, could have discovered the manuscripts that sat silently in these caves. But it was only in 1946, a year after the end of the Holocaust in Europe, when a single Bedouin boy, Muhammad ed-Dhib entered what later became known as Cave 1 and discovered the first of more than nine hundred different manuscripts that would emerge out of eleven caves near the northern edge of the Dead Sea in close proximity to Qumran. The year 1946 was also a crucial time for the British Mandate in Palestine. With the end of World War II and the liberation of prisoners from the concentration and extermination camps in Europe, streams of "displaced persons" of Europe and the former Ottoman Empire converged upon Palestine as a refuge in the aftermath of the Holocaust. In 1945 and 1946, illegal and legal Jewish immigration to different areas of the British Mandate in Palestine took place, resulting in enormous tension between Jews and Arabs The pressure to create a modern State of Israel grew as some Jews attempted to return to their homes in Europe only to discover that their neighbors did not want them to return. The cause was taken up by the United Nations, and the UN sought to create two distinct entities in the area that had been a part of the Mandate.

When I have heard religious people (Christians and Jews) refer to the coincidence of the discoveries and identification of the Scrolls, they do so with the knowledge of the timing of the creation of the State of Israel. In many ways the Scrolls helped give birth to a new national identity and the new national identity became embodied in the Dead Sea Scrolls.

WHY THERE ARE NO COINCIDENCES IN HISTORY

Albert Einstein once said that a "coincidence is God's way of remaining anonymous." Jewish history is replete with these types of "coincidences" and this fits well with many different Jewish theological views of the Divine's work in this world. What I think Einstein meant by this is that when we see events in retrospect, they fit together neatly and in organic fashion and may indeed be seen as a part of a larger Divine plan. In the ancient period, one would have called these "miracles." Miracles are sometimes defined as the events that suspend the rules of nature. While this is certainly one definition, there are many other ways that the ancients saw the unfolding of events. It is clear that some of the ancient writers of the Bible and later rabbinic Jews were not completely comfortable with this definition of miracles. The idea of "talking" animals such as snakes and donkeys (which clearly suspend the rules of nature) were not altogether appreciated by all ancient Israelites. In the rabbinic Roman period document, the Mishnah, for example, the rabbis have a tradition that God basically built into the rules of nature all of the elements that were in the text of the Bible and seemed to suspend the rules of nature. If God had built them into the system from before the beginning of time, then they were not really miracles but rather preordained events and elements waiting to be discovered.

Another Jewish view is that coincidences of history are viewed as stylistic ancient forms of writing about extraordinary events whose timing suggests that there is a transcendental force at work. Many of these elegantly timed events would be "collapsed" into a single mega-event. An example from a literature that was nearly contemporaneous with the writing of the Dead Sea Scrolls is from the books of Maccabees. There are two books of Maccabees (actually there are four books designated as "Maccabees" in many collections of the Apocrypha, but I will compare only the first two). The first two books are really telling the same basic story but were apparently authored by different Jewish authors with varying ideas about miracles. The story of the Maccabees is associated with the desecration of the Temple of Jerusalem in the second century BCE and its ultimate liberation by the Maccabees and the inauguration of a holiday celebrating the victory named: Hanukkah" (Dedication or rededication of the Temple). According to I Maccabees, in approximately 169 BCE Antiochus IV marches on Jerusalem and sacks the Temple, and two years later in 167 the city was burned, the Jews expelled, and fortifications of the city destroyed. The I Maccabees author (who does not favor the suspension of the rules of nature even for the victory against the Greeks) writes that the ultimate coincidence occurred during the final battle "on the very day that it [the Temple] had been profaned it was restored." The author of II Maccabees favors all types of miracles, including the suspension of the rules of nature to insure victory. There is the miraculous death of Antiochus IV; the Maccabean commander, Judas, is helped by supernatural beings and he leads his men to victory and purification of the facilities on the exact same calendar day as when it had been profaned two years before. What they share is the idea that a coincidence was a form of Divine intervention. For these ancient writers this was how the Divine worked. Events that were coincidences were seen as a result of some hidden Divine plan. To this day Jews recite on Hanukkah a special prayer for the many "miracles" that were wrought on their behalf at this particular time of the year. Although the Jewish sources are not in total agreement as to which miracles they are referring to, it is clear that those who redacted the prayer are collapsing a number of different sources and "coincidences" into one single prayer of thanksgiving.

So-called coincidences that occur in the process of uncovering archaeology are also well known. Few archaeologist like to write about them. Many point to coincidences that sent explorers in the direction to discover (or better, *rediscover*) ancient temples and tombs. The diaries and writings of explorers such as Hiram Bingham at the ancient Inca site of Machu Picchu, Howard Carter at the tomb of Tutankhamen in Egypt, and even Heinrich Schliemann at Troy are filled with what they considered to be a series of fortunate events that led to their discoveries. The tales of the rediscovery of Mayan and Aztec temples and cities are replete with "coincidences" that happened to the archaeologists that found these cities in far-flung jungles and rough terrain after many others had trod the same locations and found nothing. We constantly hear—in reports on the rediscovery of European cave dwellings, buried treasures in fields, and the recovery of ancient and premodern artifacts—how the people involved had been drawn to the spot by more than just informed intuition. There is a dark side to this line of thought. The discovery of the tomb of Tutankhamen in the 1920s, for example, was followed by a series of unfortunate events. These catastrophic "coincidences" gave rise to the notion of a "Mummy's Curse." The idea that there was a supernatural power at work can also unleash a Pandora's Box of energies. It may indeed just be a random series of unfortunate events, but one can understand how the events could be seen as being too connected to one another to ignore. The explanations never quite satisfy the skeptics who view a direct cause and effect in events. However full history may be of these types of incidents that look like a direct cause and effect, they can also be reasonably viewed as not direct cause and effect. It is one of the reasons why some people view spontaneous healings as Divine miracles and some physicians just see these healings as a fortuitous series of natural processes. The events of history rarely speak for themselves, and events, after the fact, can be organized in a variety of ways to show very different things.

THE "MIRACULOUS" DISCOVERY
OF THE DEAD SEA SCROLLS

The events associated with the discovery and early recognition of the value of the Dead Sea Scrolls has a series of "coincidences" that could not have been scripted even in Hollywood. The "coincidences" are worthy of study themselves and are well known to the excavators as well as to the many thousands of commentators on the Scrolls. The timing of the discovery was seen by some as the unseen "Divine Hand" (the *Deus ex machina*) reaching into history to allow a window to open on the past that was both fortuitous and significant for humanity. In many of the books, articles, and pronouncements that were published in the 1950s, it is clear that many Christians saw the discovery as more than just accidental. Theodore Heiline's book, *The Dead Sea Scrolls*[7] has an entire section in the book entitled "Timed Events," and he writes:

> Important events of this kind do not fall out haphazardly. They come to pass when the time is ripe for their emergence. They are called forth by man's thoughts, by the inner activity of his spirit, by his soul's needs. The discovery of the *Dead Sea Scrolls* is clearly such a timed event. The present religious revival and spiritual renewal that is everywhere manifest has created such a state of mind that earnest seekers after deeper truths can profit in a tremendously important way from what the scrolls reveal. It is safe to say that never in the course of the two thousand years during which they have remained hidden could their uncovering have had the significance that it has at this particular time. The questions they answer have not yet been asked so generally nor with such insistence. Today the contents of the scrolls, together with their many implications, are of first importance. Such is the tension, the inner and outer stress and strain of these terribly confused, chaotic and tragic times, that any evidence touching upon the validity of the spiritual basis whereon the Christian faith rests, is eagerly grasped by the many striving to pass from skepticism to faith. The

strengthening foundations of faith were never so urgent. So the scrolls have come to light at just the right psychological time. (29–30)

Heline goes on to say later:

All of which points to the fact that now is the "appointed time" for the discovery of ancient scrolls containing a message as important to the present generation as it was to the generation to which it was addressed two thousand years ago. (75)

Many Christians saw the discovery of the Scrolls as initiating some new countdown for the "Second Coming," or as a "message in a bottle" precisely addressed to modern skeptics and people disheartened by the inhumanity of World War II and the Cold War. Scholars and locals had other historical opportunities to discover these Scrolls in caves along the Dead Sea, but only in 1947 were they suddenly discovered and authenticated. The first major written accounts about the Scrolls that were presented to the general public saw the event as a startling postscript to World War II's Christianity in the United States and Europe. The Scrolls were a type of mild corrective to the forms of the original religion of Jesus, which had somehow, through the course of time, become something other than what it originally was intended. The Scrolls were a revelation and reformation event for modern Christians.

In the United States in the post–World War II era, American Christianity saw the need to flex its muscles as a legitimate and indeed authentic form of Christianity. Sermons and writings of prominent Christians show just how much the "footprint" of the Scrolls could demonstrate the authenticity of American Christianity. For example, Dr. Charles Frances Potter, who was a pastor of the All Souls Church (a Unitarian church) in Washington, D.C., used the Scrolls as a way to teach how American Christianity in the 1950s was the natural continuation of the ancient *Essenes* (a Dead Sea Jewish sect) in his book *The Lost Years of Jesus Revealed*.[8] Potter saw American Christianity through the lens of the Scrolls. American Christianity was something different than what Christianity had been in earlier places and times. Potter preached and wrote that Jesus was no longer the original and miraculous incarnation of the son of God, preexistent in Heaven and sent to earth as the long-awaited Messiah. He was seen as a product of his times. Jesus was the natural outgrowth of Jewish messianic views espoused by the Essenes and after the discovery of the Dead Sea Scrolls is seen as a latter-day "Teacher of Righteousness," the leader of a group mentioned in the apocalyptic texts of the Scrolls. In the 1950s, Dr. O. Preston Robinson's *The Dead Sea Scrolls and Original Christianity* found in the Scrolls many of the ideas of some of the foundational texts of the Church of the Latter Day Saints.[9]

THE *UNSEEN HAND OF GOD*
IN THE DISCOVERY OF THE SCROLLS

It was a different path to the Scrolls' acceptance within Judaism. For the most part, many Jewish scholars were skeptical of the sudden "discovery" of the Scrolls by Bedouin. There had been scandals in the nineteenth and early twentieth centuries with new discoveries of ancient Jewish manuscripts that turned out to be frauds or not as ancient as their discoverers made them out to be. But the connection between the discovery of the Scrolls and the events unfolding in Israel in 1947 and 1948 made many Jewish scholars take a second look at the Dead Sea Scroll discoveries. The "Hand of God" argument (or some would call it mythologizing) manifested itself in different ways to Jewish scholars. One of the famous coincidences (that has come to be seen as more than just a coincidence) has to do with the date of the identification of the Scrolls: "November 29." Eleazar Sukenik, a well-known Jewish archaeologist and paleographer, was an expert on the handwriting of ancient Hebrew scripts, through his work on ancient stone *ossuaries* (stone bone burial boxes). He (along with many others) had developed a system for dating Hebrew writing based upon a series of developments in the lettering systems. In the closing days of 1947, the Jewish immigrations to British Mandate Palestine had created enormous tension between the Jews and the Arab populations of Palestine. (This turned into Israel's War of Independence, which lasted until 1949). When the Dead Sea Scrolls were discovered, some scholars thought that they were medieval manuscripts of little or no value. Others thought they were fraudulent manuscripts created for profit, and others just did not know what they were. It was important to have a legitimate independent source evaluate what the manuscripts were to determine if they were of any importance, and indeed to determine what they said. But as the United Nations vote on the creation of an independent Jewish State in Palestine was about to take place, the violence throughout the country made it dangerous to travel between the Jewish areas of the country and the area where the recovered manuscripts were housed in Bethlehem. On November 29, 1947, on the very day that the modern State of Israel was sanctioned by a vote in the United Nations, Sukenik journeyed at great personal risk to Bethlehem to see the mysterious Scrolls. According to the story told by Sukenik and his son, Yigael Yadin, at the hour when the historic vote of the United Nations was announced on the radio, Sukenik was sitting in his home in Jerusalem and identified the significance of the Scroll that he was looking at as the oldest manuscript copy of the Hebrew Bible on the planet. He identified it as almost a thousand years older than the oldest then existing manuscript. At a time when the United Nations was voting on the fate of the new state of Israel he had identified the most ancient example of the antiquity of the new state. Yadin wrote in *Message of the Scrolls*: "It was a tremendously exciting experience, difficult to convey in words . . . knowing that some of the biblical manuscripts were copied only a few hundred years after their composition and that these very scrolls were read and studied by our forefathers in the period of the Second Temple."

Sukenik (and later his son Yigael Yadin) realized that on that fateful day, November 29, after the darkest moment in human and especially Jewish history (after the Holocaust and in the midst of the violence against the European displaced persons waiting in camps to get into in Palestine) Sukenik's identification gave new meaning to their struggles. Yadin's explanations are by far the most extensive Jewish expression of the semi-Divine force at work in the discovery of the Scrolls. He wrote: "I cannot avoid the feeling that there is something symbolic in the discovery of the scrolls and their acquisition at the moment of the creation of the State of Israel. It is as if the manuscripts had been waiting in caves for two thousand years, ever since the destruction of Israel's independence, until the people of Israel returned to their home and regained their freedom."[10]

As Sukenik's son, Yigael Yadin, knew better than most, just how he and his father were a part of both the rise of the modern state of Israel and the identification of the Scrolls. Yadin served as a well-known military figure and he enhanced his research skills by writing a PhD in ancient warfare. Both Sukenik and Yadin saw the fateful backdrop of the Holocaust and the rise of the modern State as inextricably connected. In *The Message of the Scrolls* (published in 1957—a decade after the discoveries), Yadin quotes his father as saying, "This great event in Jewish history was thus combined in my home in Jerusalem with another event, no less historic, the one political, the other cultural."[11] There are few examples when archaeologists actually sense they are in the midst of a "special" event that transcends just the excavation of a material culture. So November 29, 1947, was a not just the announcement of the UN partition plan that brought into existence the modern state of Israel. It was not just the date of the identification of just any ancient manuscript. These events were seen by them as a mysterious process of history in which they were participants. The battle to get the Dead Sea Scrolls for the state of Israel was complicated by all of the religious and political events of Israel's War of Independence in 1948 through the early 1950s. Other coincidences would follow. Attempts to sell the Scrolls by the Church in Jerusalem who had them in their possession is a famous story that is still being told. Attempts were made (and even some money paid to purchase some of the Scrolls), prompting the Church to put a now famous advertisement in the *Wall Street Journal* classified section in 1954. This advertisement leads us to one more coincidence in the discovery and the recovery of the Scrolls.

JUNE 1954

One last "coincidence" associated with the discovery of the Scrolls happened about seven years after the first event and again involved Yigael Yadin. On June 1, 1954, a Church in Jerusalem who held the Scrolls decided to advertise them for sale in the *Wall Street Journal* in the hopes of finding a buyer. A rather small, unassuming advertisement appeared among the other classified ads and declared that four "Biblical manuscripts dating back to at least 200 B.C. are for sale. This would be an ideal gift to an educational or religious institution by an individual or group." It just so happened that Yigael, Sukenik's son was in the United States on that day on a lecture tour and was alerted to the ad. Yadin was by then a well-known archaeologist and fully capable of understanding the significance of the Scrolls both for the state of Israel and the archaeology of the new state. The timing was so fateful that many people have written about just how opportune it was. During World War II many art works and artifacts from many museums throughout the world had changed hands and were often advertised in a very unassuming way so that a collector might find another private collector to sell a questionable item. Many of these treasures were purchased and consigned to private collections and little was known about these holdings after the purchase. If not for this coincidence, the Scrolls might have been purchased by a private collector—or worse, languished in the safety deposit box that the Church in Jerusalem maintained in New York City for the Scrolls until they were only dust. What is the likelihood that someone from Israel who knew intimately about the significance (and the location) of some of the Scrolls would have seen that classified advertisement for "Biblical manuscripts that date back to 200 B.C." on that June 1 day and understood that these were the Dead Sea Scrolls that his own father had identified almost seven years earlier? Below the advertisement for the "Biblical manuscripts" the *Wall Street Journal* had an ad for 10,000- to 18,000-gallon steel tanks and two electric welders, and below that an ad for a rental space in Knoxville, Tennessee. Reading it today, I cannot imagine that most would have picked up that this advertisement was for the Dead Sea Scrolls. But Yigael Yadin was alerted to the advertisement and history was subsequently made. Yadin realized that these were probably the same Scrolls that his father had identified almost seven years earlier. More importantly, because Yadin was a famed military commander, he also possessed the organizational skills to construct an elaborate plan to purchase the Scrolls through an "informed" intermediary and ensure that they could be easily sent out of the country and back to Israel without the seller knowing that he had sold it to the state of Israel. The use of an "informed" intermediary was a very important part of the plan, since the Scrolls needed to be authenticated by someone who could immediately tell the difference between a fraud and the real thing and the person needed to keep the selling price from escalating by letting on that it would be for the state of Israel. The price would have become astronomical (or impossible for the state to pay) had the seller known that it was the state of Israel that was purchasing the Scrolls. Few Israelis had as many connections as Yadin in the government of Israel, among world Jewry, the financial world, the scholarly world, and in strategic planning to plan the purchase and shipment of the Scrolls in a short turnaround time. We can all now sit back almost sixty years later and say that it was a well-oiled plan that was executed well, but in reality each part of the story required so many preexisting conditions to be in place as to suggest an enormous accident of history. The right person had to be the right place at the right time and have all of the surrounding conditions in place for the plan to be executed. I still marvel at the way that the Scrolls plan was planned and executed. Yadin was perfectly placed to create and execute the plan and knew the man who would become the intermediary as a trusted scholar and colleague in the New York area. Few Jewish scholars had dealt with the Scrolls in the way that this mysterious fellow code-named simply: "Mr. Green" had. This scholar had to be both unassuming, trustworthy, and able to recognize a fraudulent manuscript in a "blink" moment. Any hesitation and the plan could have fallen through. The plan was executed and the Scrolls were on a plane back to Israel the next day, where they are displayed to this day in the Shrine of the Book at the Israel Museum in Jerusalem. Yadin and others involved in this plan saw that the entire series of events was more than the sum of the parts. It was the ultimate "unseen" Hand of God in play in the rather mundane setting of a bank vault in New York City.

The "what-ifs" of history are one of the reasons why the Dead Sea Scrolls are included as a chapter in this book. Another reason is because my own discoveries at the ancient site of Qumran were themselves replete with "coincidences," which led us from our original excavations at Bethsaida to the Dead Sea "Cave of Letters" excavations and then to Qumran during a period from the 1990s to 2002 (chronicled in my books, *Secrets of the Cave of Letters* and *Digging through the Bible*). Over the past decade of studying our research, I discovered how much the Scrolls affected Western civilization and how different they were from any other archaeological discovery.

WHY ARE THE SCROLLS IMPORTANT?

I think that the Scrolls are a microcosm of the reason why archaeology can change our understanding of history in a short period of time. The Dead Sea Scrolls are arguably the most famous and significant archaeological discovery of the twentieth century for many reasons. The almost nine hundred different manuscript discoveries are significant because they pushed back the date of the earliest (Hebrew) biblical manuscripts by almost a thousand years. Suddenly, the text that was used by Jews as their primary religious document went from being suspected as a late antique text created to justify Rabbinic Judaism to a truly ancient Near Eastern text. Before the discovery (especially at the end of the nineteenth century and the beginning of the twentieth century), academic biblical studies had come to extremely disparaging conclusions about the text of the Hebrew Bible, and indirectly about Judaism. The lack of a complete, ancient manuscript of the Hebrew Bible had led some radical critics in the twentieth century to view the book as a late "pious fraud" that was used to bolster the faith of rabbinic Jews, and claim that the "true" biblical faith was that which emerged from the New Testament. The Dead Sea Scrolls gave Christians a new respect for the antiquity of Judaism and the Hebrew Bible and simultaneously made them see how Christianity had indeed emerged from Judaic roots.

The Dead Sea Scrolls contain the oldest manuscripts of a type of commentary on the Bible that is central to Judaism, Christianity, and even Islam. Without the Scrolls the fluid notion of religious ideas that were in transition could never totally be tracked. Not only do the Scrolls contain the oldest manuscripts of the first five books of the Hebrew Bible, the Torah (or Pentateuch) that the Jews use in their worship service, but they also contain works that were written by ancient Jews who were commenting on the meaning of the Torah traditions in the ancient period. Many of the Dead Sea Scrolls' biblical "commentaries"—such as the *Genesis Apocryphon*, for example—tell an entirely new story about the Patriarchs and Matriarchs that is not found anywhere else. What these Scrolls give us is a way of seeing how ancient and fluid the traditions of the Bible were in antiquity. When I read the Quran's story of Joseph and his brothers (which is a much more amplified story about what happened to Joseph than the Pentateuch gives us) I no longer wonder if amplified versions of ancient characters and events existed in antiquity. The Scrolls tell us that they existed and that we have only a fraction of the total of ancient traditions which were circulating in antiquity. Ancient commentaries on the Bible are very important for delineating ancient religious ideas as well. Commentaries on the Bible are really attempts at clarifying what is written in another text. Many modern and medieval Jews understand the storyline of the Bible through the lens of a twelfth-century Jewish Bible commentator (Rashi, for example) and rarely consider if this is the original meaning of the biblical text or just a medieval attempt at harmonizing the text for later readers. While these medieval commentators are important for pointing out religious ideas that are not always clear in the rabbinic or church traditions, they might be telling us more about the medieval practices than they are about the early traditions of the Israelites and Jews. The Scrolls commentaries give us a window into the past that allows us to compare and contrast what Jews in a much more ancient context believed. We have the first-century CE historian and commentator on the Bible Josephus Flavius, whose attempt at creating a more flowing understanding of the Bible is preserved in his multivolume *Antiquities of the Jews*. His effort can be called one of the earliest complete commentaries on the entire Bible and the post-biblical tradition up to his own times. While Josephus is a commentary of the biblical text, manuscripts of his work were carefully monitored and "updated" by the early Church, and it is difficult to know exactly whether they are all his original thoughts or whether they have been manipulated by later Byzantine or medieval hands. The Dead Sea Scrolls are something totally different. They provide the earliest *manuscript* discoveries of how the Bible was read by Jews and no one has had access to them to change or manipulate them. The other ancient Jewish commentators, Philo Judaeus, Josephus Flavius, the Aramaic language translation/commentary called *Targum* Jonathan, etcetera, are all slightly later than the Scrolls, and their commentaries have been carefully scrutinized by the many hands of later medieval scribes and censors. The Scrolls are the original manuscripts without later interventions.

The Book of Jubilees, for example, is seen as the oldest commentary on Genesis and is found in the Dead Sea Scrolls. The book is attributed to Moses, dictated by the "Angel of the Presence," and it is designated by scholars as *pseudepigraphic* ("falsely" attributed to Moses—it is not part of the canon of the Hebrew Bible, but is very ancient and very biblical in nature) and was probably written by a writer in the Hellenistic period. It shows us what Jews, over two thousand years ago were thinking about the book of Genesis. The word *Satan*, for example, appears in Jubilees (despite the fact that it is not in Genesis), and in it Satan is a very specific being. Satan in *Jubilees* is a totally independent agent from God despite the fact that this is not in the Hebrew Bible. In many ways, one of the most important parts of the Dead Sea Scrolls is that it gives us a critical part of the lost history of the development of Jewish, Christian, and later Islamic ideas of good and evil. We now know that some of the Talmudic and Midrashic descriptions of Gehennom (Hell), the Garden of Eden, and even the messianic aspirations of the Rabbis are rooted in the earlier views of the Dead Sea Scrolls. The history of ideas is an important part of history. Scholars of Religion ask how we get from the Hebrew Bible's rather limited "End of Days" scenario to the Christian New Testament book of Revelation. Without the Scrolls we would never know how it developed. Even scholars of Islam ask themselves where the highly evolved Quranic and Hadithic concepts of punishment in heaven and hell and the idea of a spiritual "Holy War" came from, and the Scrolls lead us back to an earlier antecedent.

CAN ARCHAEOLOGY REALLY CHANGE MODERN RELIGION?

Many archaeological discoveries, even major archaeological discoveries of textual information, do not seem to have had a direct effect upon modern religion, but they often they have had an indirect effect. Archaeological discoveries both in and outside of Israel have affected the study of the Bible, Judaism, and Christianity. The discoveries of Israelite cult sites throughout the Land of Israel in the Iron Age (both in the North and the South of the country) changed the way that people understood the biblical Temple of Solomon in Jerusalem. Up until the discovery of many different altars, shrines, and sites that were clearly Israelite in different parts of the country, the history of ancient Israel was guided largely by what was written in the biblical text. The biblical text spoke about the one Temple of Solomon and it was assumed that any of the other "high places" mentioned in the text of the Bible were simply decommissioned with the establishment of the Temple in Jerusalem. Archaeology has revealed that the picture was far more complex with competing Israelite altars, shrines, and temples throughout the entire classical biblical period (twelfth to sixth century BCE).

Most of the most profound influences upon modern Judaism and Christianity come from archaeological discoveries that included textual materials. The discoveries of texts related to the New Testament and early Christianity found in excavations at Oxyrhynchus, Egypt, in the 1890s and Nag Hammadi in the 1940s, for example, told a different version of the life and beliefs of Jesus and the early Christians and inevitably affected the way that modern Christians viewed their own faith. In 1896, excavations at Oxyrhynchus discovered mounds of texts. The texts were found to be fragments of noncanonical and canonical Gospels as well as Christian hymns, prayers, and letters. In 1945, a large number of versions of the Gospels were found in pottery jars buried in a field at Nag Hammadi in Egypt. The fifty-two texts were in Coptic, translated from Greek, and they record parallel versions of the Gospels that were written down in the early centuries of the Common Era for an audience who became known as Gnostics. While their theological ideas were different from those of Christians, they provide a window into the traditions of Jesus and the Holy Family. These texts found in systematic excavations are nearly contemporaneous with the manuscripts of the canonical Gospel accounts, and led some Christians in the modern period to decide that religious and theological diversity in the modern period was authentic and valid. Before these discoveries, religious diversity among Christians was thought to be the result of modern forces associated with the Renaissance and Enlightenment. With the discovery of these ancient variants, some modern Christian groups re-evaluated their own ideas with a new sense of empowerment. The Gnostic Gospels and the Oxyrhynchus texts are not usually consulted by modern Christian groups in their Church settings, but when they are cited by one Christian group or another, it is usually to demonstrate how diverse Christianity was in its origin and to justify the proliferation of sectarianism and denominationalism as a normative part of the Christian religious identity. The texts are cited regularly in comparisons between the canonical Gospels and standard manuscript readings of the New Testament and Church Father materials in some Bibles that are used for church study. The early liturgical formulations are sometimes cited to clarify one religious view or another in different denominations. This idea that archaeological discoveries can not only illuminate the understanding of the past but also influence modern religious practice has developed in the present period with postmodern archaeological interpretation.

THE CAIRO GENIZA AND ITS INFLUENCE UPON THE ACCEPTANCE OF THE DEAD SEA SCROLLS

Few archaeological discoveries have had a direct effect upon modern Jewish practice and doctrine like the discovery of the Cairo Geniza in a medieval synagogue in old Cairo. A *geniza* (a Hebrew word meaning "hidden") is a well-known repository for old prayer and holy books that are no longer usable in many synagogues. Often these texts are buried in a formal ceremony in a Jewish cemetery after first being collected in the geniza. The Cairo Geniza, in the Ben Ezra Synagogue of Old Fostat Cairo, is unique because Egypt was a crossroads of Babylonian, North African, and European Judaisms from the Islamic period (eighth century onward) and a center of medieval Jewish life. The hot, dry conditions of Cairo facilitated the preservation of many of these texts, and the Geniza has been visited and commented on since the eighteenth century. With the development of *Wissenschaft des Judentums* (the scientific study of Judaism that started after the Enlightenment, in the nineteenth century), Jewish scholars endeavored to write, and often rewrite, the history of Judaism in light of systematic research of all of the documents of Jewish life. This development marked a change in the understanding of Judaism, which up until the Enlightenment was based upon doctrinal and ideological guidelines that were strictly interpreted by rabbinic leaders. The discovery of the Geniza in Cairo also coincided with the development of new forms of Rabbinic Judaism that are generally called Reform, Conservative, and Orthodox Judaism.

The *Wissenschaft* (scientific) scholarship and the discovery of new texts that were not part of the rabbinic canon created a remarkable synthesis for modern Judaism. The Geniza became especially important in end of the nineteenth-century discussions of modern Judaism after some of the manuscripts were brought to Solomon Schechter (then a professor of Rabbinics at Cambridge University) for evaluation. The Cairo Geniza contained almost two hundred thousand fragmentary texts, with a significant percentage at nearly a thousand years old; these texts changed the way that Jewish scholars understood religious diversity in Judaism, both in ancient and modern times. In the beginning of the twentieth century, when the Geniza was not well known, two leading Jewish institutions of higher learning in the United States, the Hebrew Union College in Cincinnati and the Jewish Theological Seminary in New York developed two different attitudes toward the fragments that rapidly changed over the course of the century. Schechter came to regard the fragments as originating with an ancient sect of the Sadducees and not the Pharisees. Others came to see the Geniza as representing a proto-rabbinic group that provided a more flexible Jewish law than had earlier been recognized. These ancient texts were used by the modern movement called Reform Judaism as a vindication of some of the positions that they staked out for themselves which were different from traditional orthodox Judaism.

In 1903, after Schechter had settled in the United States, he had a discussion about the fragments with the distinguished scholar and leader of Reform Judaism, the head of the Cincinnati-based Hebrew Union College, Kaufmann Kohler. Here was the head of the historical positive school (later to be known as the Conservative Movement of modern Judaism) and the head of the Reform Movement discussing a single document. They were on the surface only discussing the ancient text of an ancient religious idea in a single manuscript, but in reality their discussions were about the state of twentieth-century Judaism and the way that a single manuscript can impact modern religion. For Kohler, the fragments were a remnant of the religious system of the Zadokites, Sadducees, Samaritans, and Karaites, which preserved ancient and elitist traditions and practices in contrast to the progressive and populist notions of the Pharisees. As much as the Geniza fragments influenced the understanding of ancient Judaism, early on, they were seen as a vehicle for interpreting modern Judaism. Conversely the understanding of the Geniza was influenced by the discussions going on in modern Judaism. It was a two-way street. The Reform and Conservative Jewish scholars influenced our understanding of the Geniza through the lens of their movements' ideological stances as much as the Geniza influenced Reform and Conservative Judaism.

Geniza materials are not just cited in scholarly works. Thanks to the widespread use of the Geonic and *piyut* (liturgical) materials found in the Geniza, they were used to determine Jewish law and practice in the twentieth century in Conservative and Reform *responsa* (replies to questions sent to rabbis, made in written form), and even affected the prayer books. The Geniza discovery paved the way for the significance of the Dead Sea Scrolls for modern Jewish movements precisely because so many scholars from the lead institutions, the Hebrew Union College and the Jewish Theological Seminary, were involved in the deciphering of the Geniza, and also the Geniza contained many rabbinic citations that were unknown from other sources. This suggested that there were textual materials that showed a richer and more complex history than is suggested by canonized rabbinic texts. When Solomon Schechter identified Geniza fragments as Zadokite fragments of an unknown ancient sect (albeit in a medieval copy), he provided the future framework for the acceptance of the Dead Sea Scrolls. The Damascus Document (or "Zadokite fragments") was an antecedent of the Dead Sea Scrolls. The Dead Sea Scrolls' manuscripts corroborated Schechter's identification, but also allowed the Dead Sea Scrolls to immediately have a pedigree (of sorts) of authenticity as a Jewish text.

The discovery of the Dead Sea Scrolls in the late 1940s, despite all of the controversies surrounding its meaning and the actual translation of the texts, did affect (like the Geniza discoveries) modern Jews and Christians in synagogues in a variety of ways. It is perhaps possible to say that without the discovery of the Cairo Geniza in the nineteenth century and its use by scholars and rabbis as an authentic expression of the varieties of Jewish practice, the Dead Sea Scrolls would never have claimed the position that they did in modern Jewish life. Beyond the sensationalism of early claims that either Jesus or John the Baptist was the Teacher of Righteousness, basic ideas of Judaism and Christianity were affected by the Scrolls. Suddenly the ancient ideas of the importance of baptism, resurrection of the dead, the observance of the Sabbath, eschatology, monasticism, rituals of daily and holiday observance, and so on, demonstrated authentic religious doctrines that in some form had been accepted by Jews and then later by early Christians.

In Christianity, the Scrolls were used by some groups as an authentic and influential voice of "pre-Christian Christianity." Dr. Will Varner, professor of Old Testament at the Master's College in Israel, and the college's director of IBEX (Israel Bible Exchange program), wrote:

> Is it not striking that soon after this manuscript [of the Dead Sea Scrolls] was composed, a child was born who fulfilled the hopes of Israel and inaugurated a new age? Although the men of Qumran were mistaken in the details of their messiah, they did expect one whose general characteristics were strikingly illustrated by Jesus of Nazareth, the Son of God and Messiah. It is not known if some early Christian brought the message of Jesus to this wilderness community. We are left only to speculate on how they would have responded to the Wonderful Child born in Bethlehem who was the Prophet, Priest and King of Israel.[12]

Christian eschatology, which during the past eighteen hundred years has developed around a set group of texts and writers (New Testament, Church Fathers, and others), suddenly included writings of the Dead Sea Scrolls (in their canon) to develop new and different Christian eschatological views (for example, millenarianists, preterists, futurists, manifestations of Protestant reform groups).

For modern Judaism, the question is: What is the impact of the Scrolls beyond the obvious contributions to our understanding of ancient manuscript readings of the Hebrew Bible, and verification of certain historical beliefs about the Jews in the first centuries before and after the Common Era? Do the Dead Sea Scrolls actually affect modern Jewish synagogue theology, life, and customs? Are they used to establish (or reestablish) ancient customs and beliefs in modern Jewish life? Do they translate into changes in modern Jewish life in any substantive way? This chapter will go on to investigate how the discovery of the Dead Sea Scrolls and their translation and interpretation by the scholars involved in their dissemination trickled down into the pulpits of American life from the 1950s onward.

REFORM JUDAISM, HEBREW UNION COLLEGE, AND THE DEAD SEA SCROLLS

Reform Judaism has a very close connection with the history of the Dead Sea Scrolls because of Rabbi Dr. Nelson Glueck's (president of Hebrew Union College 1947–1971) involvement with Israeli archaeology—especially in the southern region of Israel and Jordan where the Scrolls were discovered—and also because of his connections with the American Schools of Oriental Research (ASOR) in Jerusalem, where he served as director in the period right before the discovery. As a prominent student of William Foxwell Albright (a renowned biblical archaeologist), Glueck had worked as director of ASOR before returning to the United States in 1947 to take up his duties as president of the Hebrew Union College. It was at ASOR that the Scrolls were photographed for the first time in 1947. It was Albright himself who had declared in early 1948 that the Scrolls were the "greatest archaeological discovery of the century." Glueck's close relationship with Albright insured that he was involved in the study of the Scrolls from the earliest part of the discovery. The close connections between Glueck, Albright, and ASOR assured that the Scrolls would be a part of Hebrew Union College's legacy. In 1949/1950, the Hebrew Union College, celebrating its impending seventy-fifth anniversary with the new president Glueck at the helm, positioned itself as the most prominent American institution involved with the Scrolls by scheduling a series of distinguished learned society meetings at the College, among them the Society of Biblical Literature (SBL) and the American Schools of Oriental Research in late December 1949, and the American Oriental Society (AOS) in April 1950. Dr. Harry Orlinsky led the SBL and AOS conferences, at which there were almost a dozen presentations on the Scrolls in those years. The events received national attention. Dr. Robert Gordis, the lone scholar who participated on behalf of the Jewish Theological Seminary, spoke on the correlation between the ancient Masoretic tradition and the Qumran Isaiah Scroll. This is important since many Jewish scholars did not immediately accept the authenticity of the Scrolls. Most Jewish scholars only slowly warmed to the idea that these Scrolls were authentic and meaningful for the study of ancient and modern Judaism, while many Christian scholars were very accepting of the significance for early Christianity and modern Christianity.

The actual account of the discovery of the Dead Sea Scrolls is not the main subject of this chapter, but it deserves some mention. In 1946, the discovery of the Scrolls by local Bedouins in the area of Qumran is only the first stage. Qumran had been a well-known location from the nineteenth century onward, but the caves and the Scrolls added immeasurably to its importance. The cemetery and the ruins of Qumran were associated with the Essenes and other Dead Sea groups mentioned in the first-century writings of Josephus, Philo, and Pliny. Reports of possible ancient Scrolls in the Dead Sea region had emerged in the nineteenth century but had never been proven. The passing of the Scrolls from an antiquities dealer in Bethlehem to Mar Samuel, the Metropolitan of the Syrian Orthodox Church in Jerusalem, occurred over the course of one year. By 1947, Mar Samuel's manuscripts were known and had been authenticated. By 1949, the Scrolls were in the United States and Samuel was in search of a buyer.

Some within the Reform movement had an ambivalent stance on the significance of the modern State of Israel in the 1940s, so the appointment of a scholar with close links to the state of Israel was important. Nelson Glueck's appointment as president of HUC and his connection to archaeology in Israel does have a connection to the Scrolls' early acceptance by both the Reform movement and among many scholars at HUC. Rabbi Glueck, as president of a major seminary for the training of rabbis, rarely spoke about why he thought the Scrolls were so important to modern Jews, but it is clear that, that unlike other Jewish scholars who dismissed the manuscripts, Glueck saw them as more than just museum and archaeological artifacts. In one of the few insights into why he saw the Scrolls as so important, Glueck wrote in the *New York Times*:

> Could it be that the Dead Sea Scrolls, so amazingly exhumed from their long forgotten cave-burials and suddenly transported over the space of some twenty centuries to the attention of the world, were hailed unconsciously by myriads as a symbol of luminescent hope in an age of otherwise unrelieved darkness.[13]

In this pronouncement, he seems to be alluding to the dark days of the Holocaust, the wars of Israel, and the American post–World War II conflicts and nuclear frenzy (the Cold War and Korean Conflict), seeing the Scrolls as a form of a "message in a bottle" from a Divine hand. The idea of a "message in a bottle" is not just an idle metaphor—that these manuscripts had been placed in special ceramic holders was part of the mystery. These ceramic jars, so unusual in shape and size, were specially made to hold and preserve the manuscripts. The Scrolls in the caves may have been a library not only for the ancient group who lived on the Dead Sea and who wrote the materials, but also for future generations of survivors of the "war between the sons of darkness and sons of light." The apocalyptic group that lived on the Dead Sea (whose beliefs are chronicled in the Scrolls) feared that their holy texts—and they themselves—might not survive the "end of days" scenario predicted in those texts. In this way, the Dead Sea Scrolls are the ultimate "message in a bottle" to an unknown population. If they had been discovered earlier (which some may have been—it is hard to know), the message would not have been easily discernible, nor would the message seem so dramatically translatable to people living in the pre-nuclear age. To those who look at the discovery today in the post–World War II, post-Holocaust era, it appears to us more likely that they may have made a conscious decision to preserve them for some distant future time and not simply as a storage area.

Dr. Nelson Glueck and Dr. Harry Orlinsky both knew the importance of the archaeology and manuscripts of the Jews and also understood the state of biblical studies, which up until the discovery of the Scrolls was dominated by the nineteenth- and early twentieth-century *documentary hypothesis*. For many, the documentary hypothesis minimized the historical value of the ancient Hebrew Bible, and placed it as a relatively late invention of what could be described as "self-serving" Jewish writers in the Greco-Roman period.

The circumstances that unfolded in New York City in the late 1940s and early 1950s are, as already noted, unusual, especially because a Hebrew Union College professor played a central role in the purchase of four of the original Scrolls (plus fragments). Rabbi Stephen S. Wise, the founder of the Jewish Institute of Religion in New York City, brought Dr. Harry Orlinsky from the Baltimore Hebrew College to teach at Hebrew Union College in 1943. Orlinsky was well known in the 1940s and early 1950s because of his work on manuscripts of the Hebrew text (the Masoretic text), and he was favorably disposed to Israel in general. He was also in a perfect position to be the famous intermediary in the plan to return the Scrolls to Israel. Yadin's plan to purchase the Scrolls needed a person who intimately knew what the Scrolls looked like and could authenticate them when they were purchased. The possibility of another, less ancient manuscript being substituted at the last minute was a real possibility. The arrangements for the purchase were put into the hands of a very unlikely "secret agent," a grandfather-like, raincoat-wearing Dr. Harry Orlinsky. The diminutive, rather unassuming Dr. Orlinsky (known to the sellers only as: "Mr. Green") was non-threatening and believable in his role as a simple business man who was purchasing the items for a collection. But the amazing benefit of Orlinsky's presence there that day in the bowels of a New York bank was his ability to immediately recognize and authenticate whether these were indeed the original Dead Sea Scrolls that Sukenik had identified or just forgeries and/or other substitutions. As the esteemed Hebrew Union College professor of Bible, Dr. Orlinsky came to the Waldorf Astoria branch of Chemical Bank and Trust, examined the Scrolls, and bought them on the spot. Dr. Orlinsky related the story in a number of different publications:

> I was to assume the name of Mr. Green, an expert on behalf of the client. . . .
> I was to say as little as possible and to admit to no identification beyond
> being Mr. Green. . . . After leaving the vault, I phoned an unlisted number
> and spoke the word *lechayim*, meaning the Scrolls were genuine.[14]

D. Samuel Gottesman, a noted Jewish benefactor, financed the Scrolls purchase as a gift for the state of Israel to preserve the anonymity of the exchange and ensured that they would be sent back to Israel. In 1954, when the Scrolls were sold and spirited back to Israel, relations between Syria, Jordan, and Israel were particularly difficult. The looming threat from Egypt and the nationalization of the Suez Canal crisis were still two years off, but the Israelis were taking no chances in losing this cultural symbol of the presence of the Jews in what amounted to Jordanian territory. The plan was flawlessly executed and was seen by many as a minor "miracle" given all of the possible pitfalls.

The Scroll acquisition was finally announced only on February 13, 1955, some seven months after the famous clandestine purchase in New York. During this time period, however, Hebrew Union College and the Reform movement in general continued to discuss the importance of the Scrolls. The connection between the Scrolls and Reform Judaism has continued publicly to the present day, both in the Dead Sea Scrolls course work taught for the rabbinical school and in graduate student work at Hebrew Union College. What is interesting is how in this same time period the Scrolls helped change the relationship between Reform Judaism and the modern state of Israel and Zionism. It would have been unusual in the 1930s, for example, for Hebrew Union College and Reform Judaism in general to be as active in Israeli affairs as they became in the post-Scrolls discovery era. Years later, in the 1960s, when President Glueck was establishing the Hebrew Union College campus in Jerusalem and some of the leading orthodox Israeli rabbis were opposed to this, the role of the Hebrew Union College in the Dead Sea Scrolls story suddenly took on added importance. The Scrolls had an unanticipated and unusual ideological legacy. Beyond the technical details of the Scrolls' readings of the biblical and non-biblical texts, and beyond the theology that was present in the writing of the Qumranites (which was different from Jerusalem), suddenly there were many new versions of ancient customs that did not correspond exactly to the medieval rabbinic codes (a book form, rather than a scroll). In a strange ironic twist, the ancient texts indirectly provided the modern Reform movement with sources that validated their own differences with the modern orthodox Jewish movement. The Scrolls also allowed Reform Jews to have some of the most intense and meaningful encounters with Christian churches and seminaries on a subject that they both could claim as their own. As Reform Judaism had already engaged in ecumenical dialogue from the early part of the twentieth century in the United States, the Scrolls were just another new aspect to this fundamental tenet of American Reform Judaism. The Scrolls were featured as a part of almost every major Christian seminary as well. The fact that the Scrolls were important for theologians and the faithful is understandable. They were mostly biblical texts and they did have additional theological messages that were not explicitly in the New Testament or the Hebrew Bible. What is interesting for our purposes is how ancient history (especially an ancient history that is rewritten because of an archaeological discovery) influences modern history and how modern history and the writings of modern historians about the ancient period tend to be influenced by the modern period.

THE DEAD SEA SCROLLS, CHRISTIANITY, AND JUDAISM: HOW THE MODERN PERIOD INFLUENCES THE ANCIENT PERIOD

The sermon is a well-known and ancient Jewish art form that became a part of the Christian Church in the Byzantine period. It was transferred from Christianity to Islam as a form of combining elements from the life of the people into a religious textual reading for the week. Many thousands of sermons became famous throughout the generations as a way of informing and inspiring people through topics that were well known and contemporary. I begin by exploring Christian sermons about the Dead Sea Scrolls because there are just so many of them and they all seem to follow patterns. Jewish sermons about the Scrolls were more difficult to find, for a variety of reasons (some of which have to do with the immediate interest of Christian scholars and ministers in the obvious parallels to Christianity). Christians sermonized about the Scrolls at different periods of time than Jewish sermonizers did. The early pronouncements that made the Scrolls a "proto-Christianity," or a precursor to Christianity, were perceived by Christendom as good; then there was a wave of reaction to the claims that was seen as bad. One of the major differences was the sensation caused by the pronouncements of a Scrolls team member, John Allegro (the Scrolls team was made up of only Christian scholars for most of the first forty years of Dead Sea Scrolls research). Allegro questioned the originality of Christianity in light of the small amount of Scrolls information that was available in the 1950s, while Andre Dupont-Sommer's book, *The Dead Sea Scrolls: A Preliminary Survey* seemed to present the Scrolls and the Essenes as the "original" Christianity and Jesus as the reincarnated Teacher of Righteousness of the Scrolls.[15] These kinds of contradictory presentations caused many Christian pastors to reinvestigate what the Scrolls actually said, and it wasn't until the late 1960s that there was a change in attitude among Christian preachers.

The most impressive changes were attitudinal. American (mainly Protestant) Christians and Jews viewed each other's practices in different ways. While before the discovery of the Dead Sea Scrolls some Christians suspected that Jewish practices were inauthentic expressions of the life and times of Jesus, now manuscripts from before the time of Jesus delineated practices that were similar to and yet different from rabbinic Jewish practices that they wanted to know more about. The ideas of celibacy, vestments, liturgy, ritual meals and purity, relations between the genders, and organizational and leadership models that were found in the Scrolls suddenly gave American Jews and Christians freedom to innovate and change their own traditions in the face of evidence in the Scrolls. The "Jewish" identity of Jesus and Paul was not a homogeneous block but rather a series of different groups all attempting to understand how to carry out God's will in a new and very different religious reality of Judea in the Greco-Roman period. Even the literary form of exegesis, the explaining of a traditional biblical text in a totally new and distinctive (and contemporary) way—a hallmark not only of written interpretations that emerged in Judaism and Christianity but also of Jewish and Christian sermonizing—was suddenly laid out in texts that were over two thousand years old.

The vast majority of Jewish sermonizing probably took place throughout the Middle Ages and into the modern period at synagogue services. In fact, sermons in most Churches around the United States in the 1950s and 1960s used the Scrolls as a wonderful vehicle for teaching about how Judaism and Christianity were interrelated as ecumenism rose in interest after the Holocaust and World War II. It was during World War II that Jews and Christians came to live in close quarters with one another in the armed forces. In the post–World War II era, the sermon in the synagogue and the church became a vehicle for expressing how Jews and Christians were a part of the American fabric. In *Protestant, Catholic, Jew* (published in 1955), Will Herberg shows just how this connection had developed. Jews in the United States found themselves working together in a multireligious society that, in the main, was populated by Catholics and Protestants who shared common interests in their Churches with Jews in their synagogues.

In many Protestant denominations, the sermon came to replace the Catholic Eucharist. Its placement became the central piece in Sunday worship, exhorting the faithful to seek a deeper faith rather than simply fulfill rituals. In the 1950s, there was a prodigious number of sermons delivered by Christian pastors that included the Dead Sea Scrolls as a theme. Many of the sermons showed just how similar the formulas of Jesus's Sermon on the Mount are to many of the pronouncements in the Dead Sea Scrolls. Even without a proto-Gospel text, the idea that New Testament language is so similar to Jesus's teachings made Protestant preachers use the Scrolls as if they were Church teachings rather than pre-Christianity teachings. Most of the sermons I examined began with a New Testament proof text (or a holiday theme) and used the Scrolls as a means to interpret the New Testament or Christian message.[16]

The Dead Sea Scrolls are also used to discuss Jesus's resurrection. The Easter Holiday theme may not seem like a likely Dead Sea Scrolls comparison, but it is clear that the idea of the resurrection of the dead was one that rang true for Christians because even before Christianity we know that Jews took the concept seriously. Now it is true that there are particularly normative rabbinic texts that demonstrate the same thing, but the Scrolls have the advantage of not being rabbinic. They are Jewish and predate the New Testament, and yet they are not rabbinically Jewish.

Of course, part of the use of the Dead Sea Scrolls in Christian sermonizing is to create another mode for ecumenical common themes arguing for how theologically close Judaism and Christianity are by showing that the Jews can accept *multiple messiahs*. The Scrolls' use of the two messiahs seems to have two purposes. One is clearly to present that Judaism has an active messianic tradition for ecumenical discussion purposes. Again, the rabbinic tradition is replete with active messianic references, but they are rarely cited. Another tack seems to use the Scrolls' references to multiple messiahs to demonstrate that Jews accepted (and can therefore still accept) different messiahs. In Reverend David B. Smith's sermon, for example, on Acts 11: "I Had a Dream," Father Dave (as he calls himself) uses the Scrolls to demonstrate this characteristic:

> There might well have been room within Jewish society to accept different beliefs about different Messiahs. Look at the literature of 1st century Israel and you will see that different groups had different Messianic expectations. Most people were waiting for a warrior leader. Some were waiting for a priest. If you look at the Dead Sea Scrolls, it seems that the Qumran community, who were a group of Jewish monks, were expecting both![17]

THE DEAD SEA SCROLLS AND THE JEWS

For the Jews in the United States in the twentieth century, the sermon was a modern innovation to attract families and workers to synagogues on a Friday night (and not necessarily on Saturday morning) to talk about the events of the day in a time before everyone had radios and television sets. Sermons that were preached in Churches would not generally be repeated in a synagogue, but for the first time in the 1950s, rabbis saw the same materials that were relevant to the Jewish community in the same way that they were relevant in the Christian community. The sermon was the place for ministers and rabbis to enlighten their congregations to the week's news, wrapped into a biblical message. The Friday-night service and sermon was one of the central pillars of Jewish life and a major difference between Reform Jews and traditional Orthodox Jews, since it assumed that some Jews in America would only be able to accommodate the Friday service because they might be called upon to work on Saturdays to feed their families. Marshall Sklare's *Conservative Judaism* (1955), is a monumental study that explains the importance of the sermon and the Friday-night service.

Looking through hundreds of sermons from rabbis across America at the American Jewish Archives in Cincinnati in this period, one notes sermons on the major events of the day from the post–World War II era. There was discussion of the Cold War, the threat of a nuclear war, the beginnings of the new state of Israel, the sexual revolution, the status of women, the plight of children, wars across the world, books, movies, music, performers, politicians, innovations in the law, civil rights, Communism, and major American holidays among many other issues, but there was very little about the major discoveries from the world of archaeology. The sermon was the vehicle for discussing basic ideas and religious customs. Among the Jews, questions about intermarriage, women as rabbis and equal participants in the service, theological problems related to the Holocaust, gay and lesbian relations, Jewish-Christian relations, divorce, and the pressing needs for social justice were presented often for the first time in Friday-night sermons by far-thinking rabbis ordained at modern rabbinical institutions. In fact, I encountered very little of the archaeological world in nearly sixty years of sermons that I investigated from the 1940s to 2000. What I did find shows us how Jews and Christians were introduced to the world of archaeology and the Dead Sea Scrolls in a religious setting and not in a university setting.

JEWS WRITING THEIR OWN HISTORY
IN THE SCROLLS' HISTORY: 1955, 1957, AND 1968

There were a few very courageous and scholarly rabbis who saw the Scrolls as the "missing link" between how Judaism and Christianity converged. The American "melting pot" allowed Jews and Christians to interact in society, but churches and synagogues were still very different and foreign settings with rare moments of common dialogue. The Scrolls provided a few rabbis with the tools to narrow the intellectual and religious gap between the Jews and the Christians in America. To discuss how rabbis understood the Scrolls in relation to the Jews, I will offer examples through the sermons of a select group of rabbis that characterized many of the different sermons of the time. Rabbi Harold Saperstein, who for almost fifty years was rabbi of Temple Emanuel in Lynbrook, New York, was trained at the Jewish Institute of Religion and ordained in 1935.

Saperstein was a prolific writer and activist of the period and saw the discovery of the Dead Sea Scrolls as significant for modern Judaism. On Friday night, December 16, 1955, he preached a sermon simply titled: "The Dead Sea Scrolls." His motivation for this sermon may have been a series of different publications that had mentioned the Scrolls in 1955. For example, the writer Edmund Wilson wrote in the *New Yorker* magazine that the Dead Sea Scrolls and the Essenes "played no significant role in the development of Judaism."[18] Saperstein does not seem to have accepted this idea, and his sermon explained his belief in the Scrolls' importance to modern Judaism.

Saperstein's remarks included the elements from the Scrolls that demonstrate the close relationship between Judaism and Christianity; this was a constant motif in the Scrolls sermons that I saw. Most of the sermons that dealt with the Dead Sea Scrolls were usually placed in anticipation of Jewish-Christian ecumenical events and holidays when rabbis attempted to demonstrate the close relationship between Jews and Christians (Saperstein planned his sermon for just before the Christmas holiday; the other popular period was before Easter).

Rabbi Edward Klein (also ordained at the Jewish Institute of Religion) of the Stephen Wise Free Synagogue in New York City, in his Friday-night, December 6, 1957, sermon, titled "More on the Dead Sea Scrolls," notes:

> The authors of the Dead Sea Scrolls speak to us across two millennia of the amazing vitality and creativity of an ancient people, the rag-tag and bob-tail of the ancient world, a tiny people over-run by Greeks and Romans, able nonetheless to give humanity its God idea, its Bible, its prophets, its commandments to give more than half the world its faith. They bid Christianity to recognize a new and even greater debt to Judaism, than had before been known. On the eve of Chanukah and Christmas, the Qumran covenanters urge that Christianity and Judaism, unique in their separate beliefs, yet even closer than before in the things they share, fulfill their mission as Children of Light, doing battle against the forces of darkness.[19]

In fact, many different sermons were delivered on this particular Shabbat in December 1957 because it marked the tenth anniversary of the discovery of the first Dead Sea Scrolls.

Both Jews and Christians found fodder for sermonizing about the Cold War in regard to the Scrolls . For example, Rabbi Richard C. Hertz, the Rabbi of Temple Beth El in Detroit, Michigan, delivered a sermon on December 6, 1957, wherein he specifically mentioned how the Scrolls were a counterbalance to the scary nature of the 1950s arms race:

> In the 20th century of sputniks and rocket ballistics, it is good to gain a little perspective on the values of life and realize that there is still fascination in an ancient Jewish time, that new discoveries are constantly being unearthed. And it is also a little humbling to realize that modern man, for all his vaunted scientific and technical wizardry, still does not know everything about the long ago and far away.

The Dead Sea Scrolls did provide this opportunity for many preachers. Nelson Glueck (the president of the Hebrew Union College in Cincinnati, mentioned earlier in this chapter) observed in 1955 that the discovery was not reserved only for professional archaeologists and Bible scholars and that it had a potential influence upon Judaism in his own times. In his 1955 *New York Times* review of two books on the Scrolls (Millar Burrow's *The Scrolls from the Dead Sea* and Eleazar Sukenik's *The Dead Sea Scrolls of the Hebrew University*), which Glueck titled: "New Light on the Dim Past," he wrote: "Their very names [the Dead Sea Scrolls] excite the interest of all who are alert to the ideas and tendencies related to some of the main theological tenets of our own times."[20]

Saperstein, like other rabbis of his period, followed assiduously the *New York Times* and its book reviews, and had read Glueck's piece. On that Friday night in December 1955, he exposed the Reform Jews of Long Island to an idea that they might otherwise not have seen as subject matter that pertained to them: the significance of the Dead Sea Scrolls for Modern Jews. Saperstein wrote:

> Now what do these discoveries have to tell us about religious history—first for Jews and then for Christians. As Jews as Professor Burroughs [*sic*] of Yale Divinity School has said—there was more variety and flexibility in Judaism than we have ever before supposed. It helps us to realize that there was in ancient times in Judaism room for minority groups and freedom for minority people. But more important it helps us to know more about our own religious literature."

Rabbi Saperstein mentioned the Scrolls only once in a sermon in 1955, but some thirteen years later, he mentioned them again. On Friday evening, January 5, 1968, he preached a second sermon on the Dead Sea Scrolls. I was there on that Friday night, and while one can never say what causes one to make a decision about one's own future career, I remember being moved by his presentation. When I read the manuscript of the sermon for the first time in the *American Jewish Archives* in Cincinnati, I felt a shiver down my back remembering the specifics as if Rabbi Saperstein had spoken them yesterday. I recognized the note cards that were meticulously typed. In this period rabbis would write their sermons down word for word and usually read them exactly as they had written them. I read it and saw that Saperstein had put his finger on what I had discovered while researching the archives of rabbis and Christian preachers of the period. The Scrolls were not just a simple ancient artifact; they spoke to ancients and continue to have importance for modern Judaism.

From June 1967 onward, Rabbi Saperstein reported on the major events in Israel with particular vigor. In the years 1967 to 1969, I remember being particularly moved by his presentations of the modern life of Israel and especially the archaeology. Rabbi Saperstein held that Reform Jews were a modern continuation of the life and times of the historical Jews that extended back to the biblical world. He wrote:

> Now what is the importance for the understanding of Judaism of these greatly publicized ancient scrolls? Outside of the fascination of dealing with something which goes back 2000 years—do they throw light on our heritage? I think they do.
>
> First, they add great support on the accuracy of our current Bible text.
>
> Second, they make us realize that we are not the people of the book but the people of the books. We had come to feel that the only book that has come down from ancient times was the Bible. We suspected that there were many other books which had somehow got lost—there are hints of some in the Bible itself. But we had never seen any. Now suddenly we have come across a group of these books—each with a character of its own and can better appreciate how rich the total literary heritage of our people must have been.
>
> Thirdly, we are reminded of the great variety of Jewish religious thought and practice during the time that the Jews were in an independent nation. Judaism was never a monolithic faith. There was a great deal of free religious searching. There were many differing, sometimes conflicting groups. The break away from tradition by Reform Judaism in our day is not an innovation in Jewish history at all.

Saperstein is one of many rabbis who made the leap that the Dead Sea Scrolls, which had been purchased through the intervention of the Reform movement, really did reflect as much about Reform Judaism's emergence in the nineteenth century as it did about the Qumranite's emergence in the second century BCE. Reform rabbis saw themselves in the twentieth century in much the same way as the Qumranites must have seen themselves in the first century. Rabbi Saperstein finished: "The ancient scrolls that come from the area of the Dead Sea still have the potential of life and light and inspiration for the people of Israel. Amen."

Saperstein and many other Reform rabbis preached about the Scrolls as a reaction to the press and the local interest in the content of the Scrolls. Rabbi Ferdinand M. Isserman, of Temple Israel in St. Louis, Missouri, delivered a sermon on the Dead Sea Scrolls on March 29, 1957. It was, in part, in commemoration of the tenth anniversary of the discovery of the scrolls. On that Friday night, he conveyed what must have been the sentiment of many Reform rabbis and most Christian preachers:

It is the literary record of this community that has been found. Among them is a book of hymns. These hymn books draw on biblical sources, but they reveal the originality of the community. They did exactly what we have done. We have a Union Prayer Book. In it there is a song centered around the 23rd Psalm. It is, however, not the 23rd Psalm, but it centers about it. That is what they did too. They were inspired by biblical literature and the biblical point of view, but they composed their own songs.

The recognition that there was a possibility of composing new liturgy was not a new idea. It had been written about especially by scholars of liturgy at the Jewish Theological Seminary and Hebrew Union College. Isserman was pointing to the ability of the inspired ancient author to compose a hymn based upon the Bible, therefore having the same type of inspiration that the ancient biblical author had had. The Scrolls provided Reform Jews (especially the rabbis) a validation of their "new" Union Prayer Book and all of the corrective liturgical differences that had been going on for nearly a century before the discovery of the Scrolls.

MODERN RELIGIOUS MOVEMENTS AND THE DEAD SEA SCROLLS

Preterism is a movement within Christianity that is based upon a specific interpretation of the "end of days" scenario of traditional Christianity. *Praeterism*, meaning "past" in Latin, for this group signifies that the biblical prophecy of the "end" was fulfilled by the destruction of the Temple of Herod in 70 CE. Preterists believe this is the original view of the early Church. Differing ideas from historical Christian thinkers added to the struggle, as Roman Catholic and Protestants tried to find the "true" message of Jesus's teachings after the Renaissance, in the period of the Reformation and into the period of the Enlightenment. Among Protestants, the Dutch Hugo Grotius and later the seventeenth-century English theologians Thomas Hayne and Joseph Hall found in preterism a way of understanding their own religious identity. By the twentieth century, many preterists had only theological and philosophical arguments to stand on. The discovery of the Dead Sea Scrolls gave the preterists a new way of arguing the same issues. The loose organization of preterist churches (which is subdivided into full, middle of the road, and partial preterists) is not one single movement, but the Dead Sea Scrolls show that there was a Jewish lead-up to the types of final "End of Days" scenarios that are in the New Testament and that indirectly validated the preterist contentions.

Relatively recently, in a similar way, the Scrolls have allowed a new group of Jews and rabbis to express an interest in very different ideological and theological stances than traditional rabbinic groups. Starting in the 1960s, precisely in the period when the Scrolls were becoming known in American society, the group known as the "Jewish Renewal" began to grow. The name "Jewish Renewal" is a general term for a loose form (not necessarily a movement) of Jews who attempt to weave different historical ideas—mystical, Hasidic, musical, and meditative (drawn from a variety of sources that are traditional and nontraditional, Jewish and non-Jewish)—into a fixed set of Jewish spiritual practices that would be meaningful to the modern Jew. The movement began in the 1960s and 1970s in North America at precisely the same time that the Scrolls had become known to a wider Jewish public in the United States, and most of the terminology was adapted from the Scrolls. The Jewish Renewal Movement includes prominent leaders such as Rabbi Zalman Schachter-Shalomi, teachers, and authors like Dr. Arthur Green, Rabbis Shohama Weiner, and Arthur Waskow. The original organization of the Jewish Renewal Movement,

"The B'nai Or Religious Fellowship," which Zalman Schachter-Shalomi described in an article entitled "Toward an Order of B'nai Or" was derived from the terms in the Scrolls. Schachter-Shalomi wrote: "The name 'B'nai Or' means 'sons' or 'children' of light, and was taken from the Dead Sea Scrolls material, where the 'sons of light' go to war against the 'sons of darkness.'"[21] Schachter-Shalomi saw *B'nai Or* as a semi-monastic *ashram*-like community, based upon the various communal models prevalent in the 1960s and 1970s. By 1969, taking some elements from the developing Havura movement, the Christian Trappist tradition, and the Dead Sea Scrolls, Schachter-Shalomi founded the *B'nai Or Religious Fellowship* (now called ALEPH: Alliance for Jewish Renewal) with a small circle of students. In 1974, he ordained the movement's first rabbi. Although his community has changed over the past forty years, B'nai Or did produce a number of important leaders in the Renewal movement and in Judaism in general. I often compare it to the influence that Martin Luther King had upon other Christian preachers and Christianity in general. The Renewal movement produced the *B'nai Or Newsletter*, a quarterly magazine that presented articles on a variety of Jewish topics and Schachter-Shalomi's philosophy. The Dead Sea War Scroll may have provided the movement with an idea, but the modern battle for spiritual meaning of the Renewal movement is as fresh today as it was over two thousand years ago. Most of the associated congregations acknowledge that their followers want to use the meditative techniques present in the Scrolls in their own modern religious development. The movement is not only similar to the Qumran sect, but the followers also readily acknowledge that their original intent was to move to a desert setting to continue their group's spiritual practices. The idea that the archaeology of Qumran and the understanding of the ancient Scrolls has given these two modern movements (preterists and B'nai Or) a way to understand new spiritual practices is unique in the annals of archaeology and I think sums up how ancient history can influence modern history.

MODERN HISTORY AND POSTMODERNISM AND THE DEAD SEA SCROLLS—WHY ARCHAEOLOGISTS AND TEXTUAL SCHOLARS ARE ONLY HUMAN BEINGS

No book on history and the interpretation of history would be complete without a chapter that included one of the most significant intellectual movements in the academy in the past fifty years. The movement has changed the way that all scholars read and write history from the ancient to the modern period. The movement is called *postmodernism*, because unlike the nineteenth and early twentieth-century attempts to present information in a purely ("objective") scientific way, scholars have begun to see how historical information can be influenced by the forces of the historical period in which the scholar writes. It is not so much that scholars are biased and trying to rewrite history in their own image; it is that they cannot help themselves. It is a by-product of being human to have your own independent thoughts that are inevitably influenced by your psychological, intellectual, and social circumstances. No scholar can ultimately be an island unto him/herself. Postmodernism, a loosely defined movement in a variety of very different disciplines in the humanities and social sciences (but especially in science, history, and literature) has at its root the attempt to deconstruct the motives of modern (and even ancient) writers and to see how the writers' own education, ideas, tendencies, and biases ("cultural, religious, etc. baggage") are reflected in what they are writing . In general, it tries to qualify the thing (events in history) about which the writer is writing against the thing (event) itself. It is an extremely important movement in most historical writing, but it is rarely applied to those who wrote the Scrolls and those who write about the Scrolls for the public. An ideological bent can be seen in the translations and interpretations of the Scrolls from the beginning of the research, since almost all of the original researchers were Christians. In the 1950s, Christian writers used the Scrolls all too often as an opportunity to present (in a not very veiled way) their own theological biases under the cover of writing about ancient texts. For Christianity, the Qumranites were the precursors of Christianity. The leader of the sect, the Teacher of Righteousness, prefigured either John the Baptist or Jesus and gave their roles greater antiquity. It is well documented that Father Roland De Vaux (the head of the Catholic group that first researched the Dead Sea Scrolls) interpreted the site of Qumran to be a monastery-like settlement, which paralleled the later Roman Catholic monasteries that he knew so well. Many other Christians found the parallelisms between the multiple stepped pools at Qumran and the gatherings of the ritual meals mentioned in the Scrolls as direct parallels to the rites of baptism and Communion, and interpreted what they knew about the Scrolls in light of modern rituals. In a sense, their modern Christian identity informed their scholarly assessment of the Scrolls just as the Scrolls informed the meaning of their own modern Christian identity.

The terminology of De Vaux's descriptions of Qumran followed the medieval monastery model with a refectory (dining hall), scriptorium (library), and so on. No one doubts that De Vaux's background influenced his own interpretation of the Qumranites as either prefiguring Christianity or as proto-Christians, but the recognition that one's background influences how one interprets the data (even among "objective" scholarship) is a tenet of postmodern interpretation. Father Geza Vermes, a Catholic priest, is a classic example of how postmodernist interpretation might be viewed. In his 1956 *Discovery in the Judean Desert* he eliminates from the Scrolls' text any allusion to divorce, seemingly to set up the Qumranites as proto-Catholics, and ultimately demonstrates his own agenda through the Scrolls. He is not the only one to argue that divorce is not permitted among the Qumranites, but it is an early indication of how the debates would turn out to be influential for both modern Christianity and Judaism religious debates.

The fact that the discovery of the Dead Sea Scrolls influenced modern movements in Judaism is a little-known fact. In the 1950s, Orthodox, Conservative, Reform, and Reconstructionist Judaisms all commented on the Scrolls in their official literatures and found ways of incorporating the insights into the type of Judaism that they practice. As an example, we can look to the assessment of the Dead Sea Scrolls by Cyrus Gordon. Reconstructionism, which originated in the United States from the writings and thoughts of Rabbi Mordecai Kaplan, teaches that democratic society and its diversity should be embraced. Diversity within Judaism in the post-WWII era was a difficult element to teach. After the loss of almost half of the Jewish people during the Holocaust, the idea of diversity seemed to be a particularly difficult concept for disparate groups who had lost sizable parts of their religious life. The American ideal of equality for all is consistent with Jewish historical civilization, and Jews should help in reconstructing Judaism in the modern period through these ideals. Gordon, who was a well-known eclectic scholar of antiquity during the period following the discovery of the Scrolls, developed his own understanding of them—which seems to fit in with this view of Reconstructionism—when he wrote about the Scrolls in his article titled "The Dead Sea Scrolls":

> The Qumranites had a democratic, parliamentary government. Under priestly guidance, the majority ruled in accordance with deliberations in the community assembly. Any member who desired to address the assembly could do so after requesting and getting permission to speak. Once a member had the floor, no other member could interrupt him. Orderly parliamentary procedure, with each speaker taking his turn, is delineated in the Manual of Discipline.[22]

One of the most recent examples of this phenomenon and why it matters in our understanding of history comes from a controversy that erupted in 1990 in the Scrolls story. In the late 1980s, the slow pace of releasing the translations of the Scrolls by the small Scrolls team became a major problem both for scholars and the public. The dismissal of the Dead Sea Scrolls' chief editor (1984–1990), Professor John Strugnell, shows us just how background matters. Strugnell, a scholar who had worked on the Scrolls from almost the beginning of the effort was dismissed not for poor scholarship, but rather for something that he said which revealed how his views may taint his scholarship. The controversy erupted after Strugnell gave an interview to an Israeli reporter that was published in November 1990 in the Israeli newspaper *Haaretz*. In the midst of the transition to an enlarged Scrolls translation team that included both Israelis and Jews (who had been excluded from the original Scrolls teams), Strugnell gave both scholars and the public an insight into the importance of knowing who a scholar is. In the interview Strugnell was quoted as saying, "It [Judaism] is a horrible religion. It is a Christian heresy, and we deal with our heretics in different ways. You are a phenomenon that we haven't managed to convert—and we should have managed."[23] In what must be seen as the ultimate validation of why postmodernism is important, Strugnell was dismissed not for his poor scholarly work, but rather for his personal views that may indeed have affected his scholarship.

One might ask why his personal views were at all important. In modern scholarship we realize that scholars are human beings and their scholarship is a construct that contains their own modern views that inevitably creep into their research—even if the thing they are researching is the ancient world. This is one of the great mysteries of religion and archaeology in the modern period. Archaeology is subject to interpretation by people who come to the scholarly table not as "empty slates" but full of their own views of the world. We cannot avoid this eventuality, we can only take it into account as readers of scholarly materials evaluate scholarly arguments and balance their scholarly arguments against one another. Scholars and even an archaeologist who excavates new materials are, at the end of the day, only human beings.

The Dead Sea Scrolls, perhaps because so little was revealed over a forty-year period became a vehicle for understanding modern American religion in general, and post–WWII America in particular. Strangely enough, modern religious, post–WWII (Jewish and Christian) identity seems also to have influenced the understanding of the way we understand the Scrolls. Professor Tzvi Zahavy (in a 1992 paper at the Society of Biblical Literature conference and in his blog titled "A Post-modern Reading of Three Contemporary Historians of Hellenistic and Early Rabbinic Judaism," at the Annual Meeting of the Society of Biblical Literature, San Francisco, November, 1992), assessed the work of three well-known Jewish scholars who wrote on the Scrolls in the 1980s, and showed that the scholarship of the three may indeed reflect their own religious backgrounds.[24] According to Zahavy, the scholars and their books (which include extensive interpretations of the Scrolls)—Shaye J. D. Cohen (*From the Maccabees to the Mishna*), Lawrence H. Schiffman (*From Text to Tradition: A History of Second Temple and Rabbinic Judaism*), and Alan F. Segal (*Rebecca's Children*)—each reflected something about the religious background of the writers. Professor Zahavy demonstrates that as much as modern religion was influenced by the Scrolls, the interpretation of the Scrolls is influenced by modern religion. He attempts to show that the Jewish interpreters (like the Christian interpreters) of the Dead Sea Scrolls were guided by their own modern religious backgrounds. He writes:

> An Orthodox Jewish analysis will search for "Torah-true" ideals, emphasize ritual [e.g., prayer], focus on a textual canon, on elite rabbinic leadership, highlight internal sectarian debate and differentiation, downplay interfaith relations, ignore populist involvements in religious decision, deny the prominence of changes and adaptations based on social and historical circumstance, consider acculturation an evil, and emphasize particularism.
>
> A Conservative Jewish investigation will emphasize the analysis of family structures, democratic ideals, evolutionary change, institutional development [e.g., synagogues], communal leadership patterns, the interface of scholarship and rabbinic learning, rites of passage as opposed to other rituals, and treat acculturation as a struggle fraught with contradiction and ambivalence.
>
> A Reform Jewish approach will seek to differentiate Jews from Christians and highlight the opportunities for interfaith understanding and cooperation. It will emphasize theology in a Protestant model, acculturation as a positive force and universalism. Just how much do these three introductory surveys of the Second Temple and Early Rabbinic Judaism by three well-known Jewish scholars reflect their respective religious affiliations? Let us stipulate that all to some degree do come not only out of the

minds, but also from the souls of their authors. There is no such animal as a "neutral academic account."

If Zahavy is right, we must be very careful to look out for the influence of modern religious backgrounds of the scholars who interpret ancient religious documents and archaeological discoveries. No scholarship lives in a total vacuum. For as much as these new discoveries will influence our judgments about modern faith and archaeology, modern religious identities and views will inevitably influence the interpretation of these ancient texts and discoveries. And that is one of the great mysteries of religion and archaeology about which there is rarely any discussion. When a new discovery such as the Dead Sea Scrolls is made, it will always be subject to two levels of examination. The first, "translation," is itself a form of interpretation and not just a neutral event. We have to hope that the process will be transparent, but it sometimes is done in a closed context. The translators almost immediately form impressions about the discovery, and their interpretations will inevitably attempt to contextualize the discovery in light of other information. All scholars, while they are not prisoners to their own ideologies are, at the end of the day, human beings who are subject to their own backgrounds. The more they recognize this and deal with it, the better. We often say that history is written by the "victors," but in reality, if postmodernism teaches us anything it is that history is written by historians who may have a very wide-ranging agenda beyond the confines of the period they are writing about. When a discovery in archaeology is made, it is always going to be subject to interpretation and comparison. What the experience of the Dead Sea Scrolls teaches us about history is that one has to be vigilant about who is writing the history and why.

· *4* ·

The Archaeology of Jewish Resistance in Antiquity to the Modern Period

*W*hen I finished writing *Digging through History* in 2011, I lamented not being able to end with a discovery to inspire the reader. Since that time I have worked on thirty different Holocaust sites in Poland, Lithuania, Latvia, and Greece. We have worked in destroyed synagogues, study houses, bathhouses, sewers, cemeteries, mass graves and individual burials, homes, libraries, businesses, ghettos, and concentration and extermination camps, and we have found Jewish remains in far-flung forests, gardens. and even in lakes. This all does not sound very inspiring. In fact, it started to lead me back to a totally different conclusion. In the midst of the unraveling of civilization during the Holocaust there was a literally a "light at the end of the tunnel." As we worked on the Ponar Escape Tunnel in 2016 I realized that the "Hidden Holocaust," which I had outlined in my 2012, book was actually what saved the evidence at each juncture. All of the elements that we were able to uncover throughout the years were preserved under the ground as the locals attempted to rebuild their lives.

Over the next decade I began to include sites that told a different and very inspiring tale of courage and fortitude that seemed to be inherently linked together. It was as story of how the Jews resisted their captors in each and every one of the sites. In this chapter I attempt to show just a few examples of how the Jews fought back and why this is the greatest legacy of the Holocaust; we learn that the human spirit is not extinguished even when treated so brutally. It is an inspiring message that parallels, I think, the inspiring message that I arrived at regarding what happened to Atlantis after it was destroyed.

RETURN TO SOBIBOR 2021

Our work in Otwock and our interaction with the chief rabbi of Poland, Rabbi Michael Schudrich, created a conduit for future work, not only at Sobibor but in Warsaw, which is included here on the "Archaeology of Jewish Resistance." Our "Return to Sobibor" was a part of a much larger effort to document many different types of Jewish resistance movements during the Holocaust that resulted in "escapes" of many kinds from Holocaust-era facilities.

Our work at Sobibor continued from 2009 to 2017/2018 through the film documentation of Gary Hochman, which chronicled the excavations of Yoram Haimi and his Polish colleague Wojciech Mazurek, who were joined in 2013 by the Dutch archaeologist, Dr. Ivar Schute. The creation of a state-of-the-art museum at the site that houses seven hundred artifacts from the excavations was opened in 2020/2021 and we had the opportunity to return to Sobibor in 2021 to do more geoscience on areas that were not part of the excavations project. The camp as it was in 2008 has now been transformed by the Polish authorities, and most of the areas that we were able to survey in 2008 have been totally closed to foot traffic and covered so that the site is now appropriately honoring the burials in the camp. When we arrived in 2008 the site had an open area for park visitors where most of the dead were buried and an ash pile of cremated remains inside of a cement enclosure, and it was not clear what had happened there. That all changed by 2021, and the areas of the ash pile and of mass burials and the burning platforms were all covered by rocks, so visitors are kept at a distance from the actual burial sites.

As I have mentioned many times in my books and lectures, I tell students that archaeology is really about people and not about the artifacts. We study the past not to create a long list of objects, dates, and events, but to discover who the people were, how they acted, and why. We want to know who they were as individuals and what motivated them to do what they did. Whenever possible, our geoscience and archaeology projects begin with "witness testimony" by a survivor, either a victim, a perpetrator, or a bystander. Learning from someone who was at Sobibor is irreplaceable. I have written about our 2008 Sobibor Documentation project that included interviews with survivors of the rebellion. All of those people are no longer among the living. I returned in 2021 with "new" witness testimony, new technology that we did not have in 2008, and an idea about what we were looking for. As an archaeologist, I am always looking to the past, so when I talk of "new" testimony, of course, I mean something brought back to light through fortuitous circumstances that added to the body of knowledge. What happened long ago is not new, but new to us and to posterity. I also talk of a new idea that I think adds to the body of knowledge about the significance of Sobibor. I was interested in the uprising, but I wanted to know the details of the actual escape. The escape route, how and who actually made it out, why they succeeded, and what happened to the people that tried to escape but did not make it over the fence.

THE LADDER

There ended up being four groups of Jews involved in the uprising at Sobibor, Poland, on October 14, 1943. Four different escape results all starting from the same place.

1. Those who got out and survived the war
2. Those who got out and were hunted down and killed in far-flung villages and forests
3. Those who were killed as they climbed the fence and as they left the camp
4. Those who never left the camp and were killed in the camp after the uprising

In witness statements I heard or read about the disastrous situation as the escapees tried to get over the fence with the ladder. The original plan had been to have the carpenters dismantle a section of the fence so that it would be easier for them to go out together. In many testimonies I read that they had not dislodged a section of the fence, so everything depended upon the ladder that was put up on the fence and each escapee had to go over and down. As it turned out, the use of the fence and the ladder provided just enough cover for many to get over without being shot. If the fence had not been there, the throng moving through the area would have been mowed down by a machine gun stationed nearby. In the end, many were killed at the fence trying to escape. Some tried going under the fence, others used the ladder and some were killed in the area right in front of the gates in the barbed wire.

There were many who tried to escape and did not make it into the nearby forest. In an earlier age, we would callously have called them "cannon fodder," distractions that allowed others to escape, but they were each individuals who deserved to be recognized. Jules Schelvis writes poignantly in a survivor manuscript that 158 people were caught near the Lager 1 carpenter's shop and the *Vorlager* entrance as they rushed the fence and tried to climb over with a handmade ladder, but they were gunned down by guards or killed in the minefield beyond. While it is possible that the Nazis went through the process of retrieving the bodies and destroying their remains of those shot while escaping or those killed in the minefield, it is more likely they were left where they fell. The Nazis vigorously tried to cover up the uprising and escape. Searching for the "nearly forgotten" Jewish resistance fighters of Sobibor was the point of my return.

In 2008, before my first visit to Sobibor, I had heard of the uprising, about which I knew very little. I was fascinated by this story of Jewish heroism told by those Jews who survived the war and were able to document their experience. Since then, I have discovered that there was much more to this story than just the October 14 event, and that it stands in the midst of year of uprisings, revolts, escapes and other resistance acts that gives it more meaning. Before the "big" Jewish escape from Sobibor there were smaller, earlier escapes (and attempts to escape) from Sobibor. To me and other researchers, attempted escapes also suggest that the resistance spirit of the Jews was alive and well starting at the earliest stages of the Holocaust right up until the end. One researcher actually told me, to my astonishment, that failed escape attempts should not be counted as "true" resistance events, even when documented by multiple sources, because their impact was so limited upon the war effort. But each attempt represented an enormous effort by the participants and was disruptive to the Nazi killing machine, however briefly. Each participant was indisputably a Jewish resistance fighter.

The other escapes from the Sobibor extermination camp were mostly by individuals, unorganized and unarmed, which happened starting as early as first days of the camp's building in April 1942. Individuals like Zyndel Honigman, who escaped twice, once in April 1942 and was recaptured, and then again on July 27, 1943. The escapes continued in July 1943, and for some we have names: Schlomo Pochienbnik, Joel Kopp, and Abraham Wang. They were individual Jews; some escaped and survived the war, some escaped but were later killed outside or recaptured and brought back to the camp to be killed, and some tried but never made it out of the camp, like those who attempted in August 1943 to escape by digging a tunnel from Camp 3 only to be turned in and killed.

In 2019 I was called by the son of a Sobibor escapee whom I had never heard about. It was an unusual story, and since it was a new personal testimony from a resistance fighter from Sobibor it caught my attention. The Sobibor escapee was named Chayim Felcer. He was born in the village of Sobibor in 1927 and escaped, along with his father, Shlomeh, from a transport on the way to Sobibor Extermination Camp in October 1942, when he was only fifteen, making him an early, and young, escapee from Sobibor. His son called me at my office in 2019 and left me a message and then offered a short written testimony of his story. I later listened to his official video testimony. Chaim's courage allowed him to survive the war and tell a different story of Sobibor than any of the others I knew. We documented his story by going back to the village of Sobibor to see what remained of the village in which he was born. His story started with the Jews of the Sobibor village being conscripted by the Nazis to unload the materials from a long train that arrived in Sobibor station in April 1942. The Nazis invaded Poland in 1939, but Chayim's village life only changed in 1942 when the site of Sobibor was chosen for the camp. The Nazis infamously used Jews as slave labor, so it should not be surprising that they frequently constructed extermination camps in villages with large Jewish populations. The Nazis conscripted Jews like Chayim to help build the very structures that were going to be used to kill them. He remembers it was in April 1942, after Easter (Easter was April 5 that year), that the trains pulled up to his village. As many as twenty cars of building materials arrived, and he and the other Jews of the village were forced to unload them. The Nazis also brought Jews from the Ghetto of Wlodowa, thirteen miles away, to do the grunt work of building the camp, along with skilled laborers. After his work was finished he and his father were taken to the Wlodawa Ghetto, where they were interned. Since Chayim had been involved in the construction of the camp from the beginning, he knew more about the origins of the camp that we had been investigating than any of the other people we interviewed over the years.

Sobibor village sign. (Courtesy of Richard A. Freund, Sobibor Documentation Project)

At first, Chayim had no idea what the train load of building materials was for or what was being constructed by the forester's house and tower near his village and how it would affect the Jews all over Europe, but it became clear to him later that this was a place that was committed to the destruction of Jews, and that he had to resist it. He and his father made their escape from the train that was taking them back to Sobibor in the fall of 1942, after the camp had become an extermination camp. They heard people in his car talking about escaping as they pulled off the metal manifold in the train car they were in. On that day, as they made the slow lumbering trip from Wlodawa to Sobibor, it was raining and the guards did not see them as they slipped under the metal manifold and rolled over the side of the car and they into the high grass below. He got out first and his father followed. They survived in the forest for over two years and eventually came to the United States in the 1950s. Chayim still lives outside of Lakewood, New Jersey. When we talked about his escape, his matter-of-fact presentation made it all the more chilling. He was one of the first resistance fighters of Sobibor. These individual accounts are immeasurably important. Unfortunately, for every one we collect several more are lost to the passing of time. It is only these acts of personal courage and a willingness to share the testimony that reveal that essence of what I started to discover about Jewish resistance. The resistance was not an anomaly; it was a ubiquitous pattern that could be found in almost every site we visited.

TRACKING THE ESCAPE FROM SOBIBOR IN 2021

On October 14, 1943, three hundred of the more than six hundred Jews interned at Sobibor broke out of the camp, killed twelve guards, and escaped through the front gate:

> An estimated 600 prisoners tried to get away. Due to the jostling at the gate many tried to climb across the barbed wire fencing. Some got caught in it; others who managed to get across were killed by the exploding mines. Only a few prisoners followed the plan and detonated the mines using bricks and pieces of wood. But there was not enough time and many prisoners wanted only one thing: not to spend another second in Sobibor, even if they had to pay for their flight with their lives.

Most were killed as they left the camp. Dutch historian Jules Schelvis estimates that 158 inmates perished in the Sobibor revolt. A further 107 were murdered either by the SS, Wehrmacht, or Orpo police units pursuing the escapees into the forest. Approximately forty-seven survived the war.

Little work has ever been dedicated to searching for what I call the "forgotten resistance fighters of Sobibor"—those who may be buried where they fell on the afternoon of October 14 as they tried to leave the camp. When I started at Sobibor, I was told that it was a unique and unprecedented resistance event. What I have discovered over the past decade is that it was part of a larger pattern of resistance that was centered at ghettos, concentration camps, labor camps, in forests and cities and small villages. Rather than being an anomaly, Sobibor is a part of a larger pattern of resistance behavior that the Jews throughout Europe displayed.

We returned to Sobibor to document the escape. Even in 2021, there was little indication of exactly where the escape took place. There

are no monuments to them, no signage showing where they fell. We strongly suspected that the escape happened near the carpenter's hut on the south end of the camp. The 2021 drone photogrammetry of Sobibor is made up of thousands of photographs stitched together of the site; the train tracks run down the center of the photograph and the red box is the *Vorlager* and Lager/camp. At the site of the extermination camp, there were fewer mines than at other points around the fence. It is also the location of the carpenter's shop, where the Jewish prisoners were able to build and store a ladder that helped them get over the barbed wire fence.

Drone photogrammetry of Sobibor. (Courtesy of Colin Miazga, the Resistance Project 2021)

Prior to our study, no excavations or research had been done. We were given permission to do a Ground Penetrating Radar study of the area by the Director Tomasz Kranz on July 26, 2021, to see whether there was any particular evidence of the escape and presumably to locate the Jews who were killed as they left the camp. The results of the GPR were compelling. They show a trench-like mass grave along the old fence line. It suggests many bodies were quickly and superficially buried here. Our recommendation to Rabbi Schudrich was to place some marker in this area of what appears to be what I would call a "memorial to the forgotten resistance fighters" of Sobibor—those who attempted to leave on October 14, 1943, but did not even make it beyond the camp's walls. It is inspired by some words that I had heard Rabbi Schudrich say about the victims: "Everyone deserves a memorial."

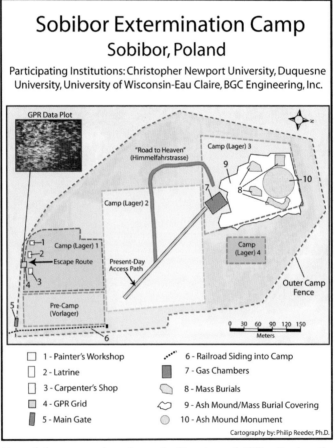

Map of the escape from Lager 1. (Courtesy of Philip Reeder, the Resistance Project 2021)

CHANGING THE VICTIMHOOD NARRATIVE
OF THE HOLOCAUST

This chapter is a corrective to the narrative of Jewish victimhood that most students encounter when studying the Holocaust. In fact, as I shall attempt to make clear with a wealth of historical evidence, Jews were not always perceived as passive victims. For millennia, Jews had a reputation of being radicals and rebels, and in the face of oppression, they always resisted. The Jews were the rebels of antiquity. Then, following the ultimate defeat of Judea by the Roman emperor Hadrian, we hear little about Jewish revolts or rebels. From that point forward, Jewish history was written through a "lachrymose"[1] lens of victimhood of the Jewish people. My team has spent the better part of three years investigating sites that demonstrate just how widespread the practice of Jewish resistance was in most areas where Jews were incarcerated. Our work is attempting to change an intellectual template that sees the Jews as victims and to demonstrate that Jewish resistance during the Holocaust was neither negligible nor nonexistent. I also hope to make clear that resistance comes in many forms.

THE JEWS WERE THE "PEOPLE OF RESISTANCE"

The Jews have been known as the "People of the Book" for millennia, but in the ancient world, and in the vast majority of the accounts in the Hebrew Bible, they are the "People of Resistance." Especially in those texts considered to preserve the earliest historical traditions of the Patriarchs and the Matriarchs, the Bible employs every literary tactic to tell a story of Jewish self-survival in a hostile larger pagan world. The texts reveal unabashedly the spiritual revolt of Abraham against his own faith, then rebelling/arguing against his "new" God when he felt that the Divine was not just. The Hebrew Bible contains ancient Israelites battling with this God and God's representatives, even as they are brought out of servitude by the "hand of God." We find the Israelite leader Moses expressing his own independence from his new identity as a prince of Egypt to be a part of the minority Israelites. We have the revolts of the Israelites against the Egyptians led by Moses, Aaron and Miriam's clash with Moses, and the accounts in the books of Joshua to Judges, of David's struggles (1000 BCE) against the tribal traditions of the people of Canaan. At the same time, we have internal battles of the Israelites and the Judeans among themselves and a two-hundred-year civil war. Even the Persian opportunity to return to their land in the sixth century BCE is greeted with resistance by the Jews in Babylonia. By the time the Book of Maccabees arrives at the second century BCE revolt against the Greek Seleucids led by the Hasmonean family of Judah Maccabee, the fact of Jewish resistance is a fixed element in Jewish literature. It appears, as well, in the Apocrypha and Pseudepigrapha with books including the names of famous rebels, and it is paralleled by a debate among the Jews of what Jewish leadership should be. With the writings of the period we see that within the Jewish ranks there are those who opted to found their own resistance communities along the Dead Sea. By the first century CE revolt of the Jews against the Romans, led by the Zealots, the theme of Jewish resistance is defined by a very specific internal battle among the Jews about what constitutes authentic Jewish identity. The existence of both Jewish and non-Jewish literary traditions in this period allows us, by the time of the second century CE revolt of the Jews against the Romans led by Shimon Bar Kokhba, to understand that Jewish resistance is seen as a characteristic of the Jewish people outside of their borders and into the Diaspora. The entire weight of the Roman empire under Hadrian is brought to bear on the revolt of an obscure people in a tiny, far-flung part of the empire in the second century. The archaeology of this period is replete with not only the literary documentation of the events, but also with examples of artifacts that tell us about the Jews of these periods.

A SHIFT IN PERSPECTIVE: THE LACHRYMOSE HISTORY OF THE JEWS

For the most part, I find that modern historians know much more about the "lachrymose" history of the Jews than the "resistance" history of the Jews. It seems to me that the changeover began in the late Roman period but continued through the Middle Ages. One artifact tells us about how the Roman world put an end to the resistance definition in a specific way. For almost a quarter of the first and second centuries CE, the Roman Empire circulated coinage that simply said: *Judaea Capta* ("Judah has been captured"). The *Judaea Capta* coins were struck originally under Vespasian, and continued to be struck by his two sons who succeeded him as emperor, Titus and Domitian, and after. These coins commemorated the capture of Judaea under Titus's command and were issued in bronze, silver, and gold by mints in Rome and found throughout the Roman Empire and in Judaea itself. They were issued in every denomination, and at least forty-eight different types are known. Judaea (which forms only a small piece of modern Israel) was a small province with a small population at the farthest reaches of the Roman Empire.

Nevertheless, the domination of Judaea was so significant that it warranted memorialization on the money of the empire. For that reason, the very word *Jew* was almost synonymous with the word *rebel*, and not rebel as just cultural or spiritual orneriness or stiff-neckedness: it was armed rebellion. Yet it was not only armed rebellion. The sites of armed rebellion were also sites of un-armed resistance that were so ubiquitous that they were almost overlooked.

MASADA'S JEWISH RESISTANCE AS A MODEL AND A WARNING

Masada was the last mountain stronghold of the Jews in the Judean wilder-ness by the Dead Sea. It was to Masada that the Zealots retreated after the rebellion of 66–70 CE against the Romans had ended in total defeat, includ-ing the destruction of the Temple and Jerusalem and the exile of many of the Judeans. The only historical source for this Jewish resistance event of the first century CE, for which there is abundant archaeological evidence, is a literary account written by defeated Jewish general, Josephus Flavius, who was never at Masada. The Jewish resistance at Masada in 73 CE, as it is recorded by Jo-sephus, seems to be, however, the model for Jewish resistance throughout the centuries since, even if the Jews themselves were not all reading about it in the writings of Josephus. In Josephus's account of Masada, I see two totally dif-ferent types of Jewish resistance presented at the same time. One is an armed rebellion, and the other is the documentation of the crimes of the Romans. For the next two thousand years, the Jews at times fought their enemies, but more importantly, documented their enemies' crimes.

Josephus's multivolume *Jewish War* and *Antiquities* are classics today, but in antiquity and in the Middle Ages they were not viewed as part of the Jewish canon of literary classics. Josephus was seen rather as a "turncoat" of sorts. At age twenty-nine, he had been appointed general of the Jewish forces in Galilee. He was eventually captured at Jotapata by Vespasian, who was at that time the supreme commander of the Roman army. Upon Josephus's capture, he was given the choice of death or conscription to the Romans to write the history of the Jews for the Romans while sitting comfortably in Rome. He chose the latter. Josephus capitulated and sought to ingratiate himself with the Roman general, eventually becoming part of the imperial court in Rome. He was an eyewitness to the destruction of Jerusalem and the Second Temple by the Roman army in 70 CE. He spent the rest of his life in Rome pursuing his literary career, the surviving results of which constitute a vital source of historical information, but which, it is suspected, was written to present to the Romans with what they wanted to read—more like Tom Clancy than Robert Cato. As much as it has told us about the life and times of the Jews and Jewish beliefs from two thousand years ago, it showed for the Roman reader how the Romans had defeated a noble and ancient people. No Roman really knew how small the province was, nor how underequipped the armies of Judea were. It was an opportunity to show the greatness of Rome, and it served the end goals of the Romans. What is significant is that it was not pure propaganda. It preserved a snippet of the ancient civilization of the Jews. Josephus must have feared the very existence of Judaism was at stake when he saw the results of the Roman war against the Jews in 66–70 CE, and he wrote to preserve what he could, but he was also compelled to write what was meaningful to the readers, which in the case of Josephus was the Romans. As well as documenting the ancient traditions and culture of the Jews, he was the first to document Jewish resistance and the Romans' cruelty and destruction of the Jews. In some ways, Josephus was continuing to resist the Romans through his writing.

His goal was not to write "history" the way we do today, but rather to collect materials that would show future generations the greatness of Rome, and, conversely, how heroic and courageous the Jews were in the eyes of the Romans. He wanted the Jews to be seen as having lived and died in a way that would make their Roman captors feel that they were a dignified people worthy of the Roman pursuit, capture, and effort expended to destroy them. Josephus says that not all of the Jews died on Masada. There were survivors who were brought to Rome to have Josephus take their testimonies. The resistance movement was documented for the first time in Jewish history by testimonies, and recorded as a part of the very document that indicted the cruelty and tactics of the Romans. We have the testimonies (whole speeches that were obviously documenting the Zealot resistance) at the same time that we have Josephus, who was documenting in plain sight his own resistance. The most famous speech is by Elazar Ben Yair who was the leader of the Zealots:

> Since we, long ago, my generous friends, resolved never to be servants to the Romans, nor to any other than to God himself, who alone is the true and just Lord of mankind, the time is now come that obliges us to make that resolution true in practice. And let us not at this time bring a reproach upon ourselves for self-contradiction, while we formerly would not undergo slavery, though it were then without danger, but must now, together with slavery, choose such punishments also as are intolerable; I mean this, upon the supposition that the Romans once reduce us under their power while we are alive. We were the very first that revolted from them, and we are the last that fight against them; and I cannot but esteem

it as a favor that God hath granted us, that it is still in our power to die bravely, and in a state of freedom, which hath not been the case of others, who were conquered unexpectedly. It is very plain that we shall be taken within a day's time; but it is still an eligible thing to die after a glorious manner, together with our dearest friends.[2]

This is considered one of the great rebel speeches of all time. One wonders whether this speech is what was actually said, or rather a creation of Josephus. Regardless, some stories are so good they deserve to be true.

Although the legend of Masada had been known for millennia, and the rock had been identified by modern explorers near the beginning of the nineteenth century, it wasn't until Professor Yigael Yadin of Hebrew University undertook serious archaeological exploration in the 1960s that the ancient fortress began to reveal its secrets to science. Dr. Yadin saw the resistance of the Jews at Masada in nearly every area of the excavations. A thing as simple as burnt grain in broken jars in the storehouses contained layers of symbolism as evidence of resistance. The Jewish rebels who died on the mountain top had left the burnt food for the Romans[3] so they would find evidence that they could have held out for months. Almost two thousand years later, Dr. Yadin was finding it again as evidence of the Jewish resistance.

The quotation from Josephus of the end of the rebellion is one of the most dramatic in all Jewish history. Josephus writes:

> They then chose ten men by lot out of them, to slay all the rest; everyone of who laid himself down by his wife and children on the ground and threw his arms about them, and they offered their necks to the stroke of those who by lot executed that melancholy office; and when these ten had, without fear, slain them all, they made the same rule for casting lots for themselves, that he whose lot it was should first kill the other nine, and after all should kill himself.

Yadin's excavations revealed a collection of inscribed ostracons, or pottery shards, with a series of eleven (or more) names in a room off to the side of the main mountain village, and he interpreted it as the place where the lottery[4] was conducted. He took Josephus at his word.

Noble suicides, martyrdoms, and dignified deaths were a characteristic that would have made a big impression on the Romans who read Josephus. I remember the first time I read about the Ben Yair pottery shard and the story of the ten chosen fighters who went out to kill all of the Jews before they were carted away to Rome as slaves. I realized that all of the people on Masada had died, but the writings of Josephus remained as the strongest expression of Jewish resistance by documenting the event. It was at that moment that I realized that the pen is mightier than the sword. The Romans passed from the scene, but the story lives on. The Jewish resistance recorded by Josephus remains as the single most powerful indictment of the Romans and expression of Jewish resistance.

Most non-Jews do not know that the story of Masada is not really a part of Jewish liturgy. The stories of many other similar martyrdoms have been a part of Jewish liturgy read on the High Holidays in synagogues around the world for at least the last six hundred years. In the Middle Ages, Jews resisted their Crusader captors by taking their own lives before being subjected to the degradations of imprisonment and slavery. Throughout much of my childhood (and adulthood), I would read all of the martyrologies of the Jews, which make up a significant part of the Jewish commemoration of Yom Kippur, and wonder what they called upon me to do. Was I to give my life up rather than suffer the indignities of my captors, or was I to tell the world about the crimes of the attackers? These liturgical poems follow the medieval attacks against mostly European Jewish communities, but also accounts from the Mediterranean, Middle East, and North Africa. During the Yom Kippur service, Jews read the poetic accounts of excess against Jewish communities, some of which date from eighteen hundred years ago, and we see that these Jews did not or could not take up arms against their attackers, but they did compose elaborate accounts of what happened to them. That sense of cultural preservation through documentation has always impressed me. I find that the value of the nontraditional forms of resistance, not the fight or flight forms, have been overlooked by most people assessing Jewish resistance throughout history. Their value has impressed me with its significance as I study the Holocaust with geoscience and archaeology.

ARCHAEOLOGY AND ETHNIC MARKERS

I remember the first time that I was excavating a site and started to recover only pieces of animals that were considered kosher (cows, goats, and sheep) and no sign of animals that were not kosher (most commonly, pigs), and I realized this was an ethnic marker for Jews, since in a site nearby they were many pig bones. Over time, archaeologists have developed a whole series of ethnic markers to help identify ancient sites that might otherwise not be distinguished by literary accounts.[5] Since our work is about identifying specifically Jewish remains, the following list of markers gives you an idea of how we can read a site. Dietary "trash" of kosher and non-kosher animals is significant. It is usually statistically determined, since we assume that even at a Jewish site we will find varied populations of people, some who observe and some who do not observe dietary laws. Coins, pottery, glass, and metals and even specific types of decorations on a whole variety of artifacts are very revealing. Obviously, writing is a huge marker when we find it. There are ancient and later versions of Hebrew. The stepped ritual bathing pools known as mikva'ot are another ethnic marker that can be found in Jewish sites in ancient Israel and the Diaspora. The use of caves, hideaways, or escape tunnels are found in many Jewish sites in ancient Israel and the Diaspora. and it is something that seems to have provided a very specific purpose during periods of relative peace and during war.

The use of these ethnic markers for defining a site is not an end in itself. They aid in understanding a site both in antiquity and in the modern period with regard to how the people conducted themselves at that moment, and how that conduct changed or did not change over thousands of years. These ethnic markers can help define issues in Jewish history beyond just religion. They are prevalent in sites around the Dead Sea Scrolls find, where Jewish resistance was centered for almost three hundred years from the Greek period through the Roman period.

The Origins of The Resistance Project

Once we started looking at many different Holocaust-era sites, I started looking for Jewish resistance markers at those sites. Certainly, armed uprising was a marker of resistance. The Warsaw Ghetto, Sobibor; these were obvious. Were there others? At the Ponar burial pits outside of Vilna, which we worked in 2016, and which is documented in my book *Archaeology of the Holocaust* (Rowman and Littlefield 2019), we discovered an escape tunnel that few believed existed, despite it appearing in numerous survivor testimonies. Many thought it was a fantastic story told by survivors to bolster their reputations, since those survivors had been forced to perform unspeakable acts. I myself was skeptical of the tunnel's existence prior to discovering it, because I had been brought up in Hannah Arendt's reality to see Jews as victims rather than as courageous resistance fighters during the Holocaust. I could not even imagine how those Jewish prisoners could have dug a 100-foot-long escape tunnel with their hands and rudimentary artifacts such as spoons and metal pieces. As a scientist, my methodology is to take the testimonies seriously. We had multiple testimonies by survivors who described the tunnel's excavations. We began with that. We looked for the route. We traced the details of what they said they did. To the dismay of many, we discovered the tunnel. Suddenly, within months of this discovery I had survivors writing to me about many different escape tunnels that they remembered from their experiences in the Holocaust. This was an ethnic marker of Jewish resistance during the

Holocaust, which of course has appeared over and over again throughout Jewish history.

At HKP 562, a labor camp on the outskirts of Vilna, we uncovered hiding places, or *malines*, in the barracks used to house the Jews. Survivor accounts told of how the Jewish prisoners constructed these locations. We had people writing to us about how they had hiding places inside their homes, their barns, their neighbors' homes, their businesses, as well as obscure places in the forest, caves, bunkers, and churches, and all told the same story. At scores of places we were directed to help uncover small and large hiding places that Jews had used to evade the Nazis. Hiding places became another ethnic marker for Jewish resistance in the Holocaust. Now I had three ethnic markers: armed and unarmed uprisings, escape tunnels, and hiding places.

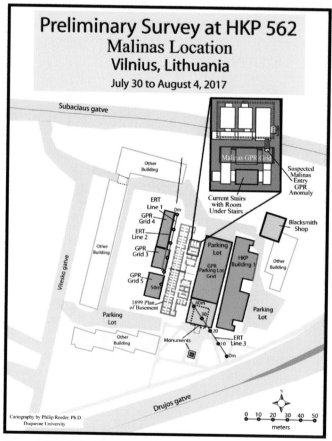

Map of HKP 562. (Courtesy of Philip Reeder, Good Nazi Project 2017)

I started to notice small elements of the testimonies that suggested two other very prominent but largely ignored forms of Jewish resistance in the Holocaust. The testimonies were replete with stories of religious devotion that included rabbis risking their lives to save religious books, to perform prayer rituals, to attempt religious teaching and services, to bury the dead, eat a piece of matzah on Passover, to light a candle on a holiday, and to perform a religious act that added to their daily routine. Many did these acts at the risk of their lives. In addition to the spiritual resistance that was done by pious Jews and rabbis, I found musicians and cantors; poets, writers, and playwrights; and artists who practiced their own form of resistance by creating works that were often couched in metaphors and allegories but allowed these artists to resist the Nazi propaganda with a seemingly innocuous message that inspired the group who truly understood them. In many ways, these cultural ethnic markers provided a post-Holocaust corpus that shines a light on this spirit every time we read, see, or hear these works.

Many Jewish resistance fighters kept journals, gathered notes, and created archives, intent upon saving information about the conduct of the Nazis and their collaborators in the off chance that the documentation would provide a witness for future generations. In fact, documentation may have been one of the most powerful forms of resistance, since many of these records served to indict the Nazis for their behaviors during the Holocaust and at the postwar trials.

Now I had a foundation for study, and the search for these is my *Resistance Project*. I had five markers for Jewish resistance during the Holocaust, each appearing throughout history in times of Jewish struggle against oppression. *The five categories of Jewish resistance are: fight, flight, dissimulation, devotion, and documentation.* When I speak of fight, I mean armed and usually organized resistance. The example of the Warsaw Ghetto uprising is perhaps the most famous, but it is only one of several. When I speak of flight, I mean unarmed escape, whether organized or merely fortuitous. The escape from Fort IX in Lithuania is one example I shall return to later in the chapter. Dissimulation is the act of going into hiding in any form. I share in this chapter the poignant stories of several "hidden children." Devotion is the preservation of Jewish history, culture, and identity through all manner of expression, including the creation of prayer locations, prayer activities, art, music, plays, and literature. As just one example, I discuss the Ringelblum archives later in this chapter. Finally, documentation is the use of written material to record the crimes of the Nazis and their collaborators, and can include items preserved during the war as well as transcribed testimonies taken from survivors after the Holocaust. These five different forms of regular and often daily resistance are all found during the Holocaust, often happening at the same time. There was no single Jewish resistance organization or leader in the Holocaust. Resistance was a natural extension of the duties of living a Jewish life, only done in a period of extremis.

WHY JEWS DID NOT GO TO THEIR DEATHS "LIKE LAMBS TO THE SLAUGHTER" DURING THE HOLOCAUST

Holocaust is not the preferred term to describe the events that happened to the Jews during World War II. The term *Holocaust* was developed by non-Jews after the war, and is Christological terminology that runs through the work of most theologians who attempted to explain the attempted genocide to themselves and others in the post–WWII world. The term borrows from the trauma that Christians feel about the death of Jesus. In Christian theological discussion, "Christ" is the "lamb" that was traditionally used in Temple period sacrifices. Thus, when comparing the wanton destruction of the Jewish people during the Holocaust, the "lamb" image is very prominent in the minds of Christians. For many Christians, the death of Jesus has meaning if it is part of some theological scheme that God has for the world. So too, the death of so many Jews, those who were non-combatants, in the heart of European Christendom can only have meaning if it is part of some theological plan. To Christians, Jesus died so that "you" could be saved. When trying to unpack the meaning of the killing of six million Jews in the midst of Christian Europe, Christians wrapped themselves into a Christological package that is intelligible to them to give meaning to an unimaginable act of horror and murder. Thus, accepting one's fate and not resisting is seen as a virtuous act, at least to Christians.

The second Christological idea that is found in many early writings about the Holocaust is that the Jews of the Holocaust had gone to their deaths like lambs to the slaughter. "Sheep to the slaughter" is often a way of explaining the death of Jesus on the cross as accepting the Divine plan. As "sheep to their [Divine] shepherd," Paul writes in the Letter to the Romans 8.35–37: "Who shall separate us from the love of Christ? Shall trouble or distress or persecution or famine or nakedness or danger or sword? As it is written: For Your sake we face death all day long; we are considered as sheep to be slaughtered. No, in all these things we are more than conquerors through Him who loved us." Many Christians feel that it is actually a positive idea that the Jews went to their deaths like sheep to the slaughter. Heroic martyrdom is indeed a religious value in Judaism, and "living and dying for one's beliefs" is a form of Jewish resistance. While moments of heroic martyrdom can be found in the Holocaust, this cannot be applied to all, or even most of what happened.

The term *holocaust* in the Bible means a "wholly burnt sacrifice," and is an allusion for theologians to the "burning of the bodies" at extermination camps and elsewhere. The word *holocaust* is found many times in the King James English translation of the Bible. It is not only the use of the biblical word *holocaust*, but also the notion that the sacrifices were somehow a compensatory offering for some type of sin that makes the term so problematic. The Jews who emerged from the death camps called what happened to them *Der Churban* ("Destruction" in Yiddish). The term *Holocaust* suggests that the ancient Israelites needed to give this sacrifice to God for something they had done. The Jews did nothing to warrant the Holocaust nor did they see this killing and death as salvific in any way. I tell my students that Jews prefer the term *Shoah*, a neologism (but the Hebrew root is found in biblical texts), to describe a unique event of destruction without trying to assess why it happened. *Shoah* is simply destruction without meaning. *Churban* is a term that had been applied to the major destructions of ancient Jewish history, for example, the Destruction of the Temple of Jerusalem in 586 BCE and then again in 70 CE. It just so happened that we began our work in the summer of 2021 on July 18, which is the commemoration of Tisha Be'Av, the 9th of the Hebrew month of Av when both Temples of Jerusalem were destroyed. The destruction of the Temples happened during wars in which the Jewish soldiers fought against the Babylonians in the sixth century BCE, and the Romans in the first century CE, so even the destructive acts of these periods do not really accurately compare with *Shoah*. The *Shoah* was not like the *Churban* of the Temples, nor was it a sacrifice; it simply was destruction.

THE ARCHAEOLOGY OF JEWISH RESISTANCE DURING THE HOLOCAUST

I have worked many Holocaust sites during my career. While each site is unique, it is still true that there are similarities and patterns visible among the many sites. It became clear that we were seeing sites that were inevitably connected back to forms of Jewish resistance that were not registering in other collections, or that had been so separated from one another that each form of Jewish resistance was seen as an anomaly. Jewish resistance during the Holocaust is still not a major topic in Jewish history books. Many books mention resistance, and there are groups that celebrate the Jewish partisans, individual uprisings (especially the Warsaw Ghetto Uprising) and revolts.

There are also commemorations of spiritual, artistic, musical, cultural, and literary events during the Holocaust. Mostly, these events are treated as "window dressing" during the Holocaust rather than as full-fledged attempts to defeat the Nazis. I maintain that these are all legitimate efforts of resistance. Cumulatively, these events, celebrations, and commemorations form a body of work that is hugely significant. It is essential to view them as a whole, rather separated into individual moments. Collectively, they give the Jews a posthumous victory over Nazism after the Holocaust. Also, when you put them all together they appear ubiquitous, as in fact they were.

My geoscience and archaeology group has committed considerable resources over the past five years, but especially in the last three years, to collect data about resistance sites to tell more about this story. I was looking at the tens of thousands of photographs that we have amassed in our different projects and settled on a photo of a broken fence at Sobibor to depict the archaeology of Jewish resistance during the Holocaust. It is not a picture of a gun or a mass grave, but an artifact that kept the Jews interned and that, in the end, serves as a symbol of what continues to be the evidence of the Nazi "crimes against humanity."

JEWISH RESISTANCE AT AUSCHWITZ

Surrounded by thousands of SS troops, under the tight control of local and armed Nazis, the most unlikely place for Jewish resistance during the Holocaust was the extermination camp known as Auschwitz-Birkenau. By 1944, the Nazis required as many as nine hundred *Sonderkommandos* to process the numbers of Hungarian Jews who arrived there every day. Unlike the Sonderkommandos of Ponar and Fort IX who survived the war, those from Auschwitz-Birkenau were not generally hailed as heroes, but were instead ashamed of their work and rarely talked about their experiences. Why? Part of the answer lies in the fact that the Nazis chose Greek Jews (mostly from Thessaloniki, Rhodes, Kos, and other islands) who were ethnically different than the vast majority of the inmates at Auschwitz. They spoke Ladino, a Jewish language completely distinct from Yiddish, which they neither spoke nor understood, and they did not share the Ashkenazic customs of the vast majority European Jews at Auschwitz. Sonderkommandos were also disliked by the other prisoners, in general, for accepting the meager extra benefits accorded them. Even though all of the prisoners at Auschwitz knew that the work of the Sonderkommandos was grueling and dehumanizing and that Sonderkommandos were cycled out of this task on a regular basis and frequently executed after completing their tours, the Sonderkommandos nevertheless became, like the leaders of the Judenrat, an easy target to blame for the terrible life of the prisoners in Holocaust camps and ghettos. On October 7, 1944, several hundred Sonderkommandos responsible for Crematorium IV rebelled, killing three SS guards and torching the crematorium. We know about this because we have written testimony from at least one eyewitness. The tale of how this testimony came to light is both poignant and extraordinary.

Sonderkommando Uprising site. (Courtesy of Richard A. Freund, the Resistance Project, 2021)

THE SCROLLS OF AUSCHWITZ

Marcel Nadjari, a Greek Jew from Thessaloniki, was a Sonderkommando at Auschwitz. He participated in the planning and in the rebellion on October 7, 1944. Miraculously, he was not murdered by the Nazis when the rebellion was eventually put down, and he survived the war, returning to his native Greece for a time before eventually moving to New York, where he died in 1971. While at Auschwitz, he wrote a journal of several pages,[6] recording in detail his observations of life in a death camp, including details of the October 7 rebellion. He placed this journal in a thermos[7] and buried it near Crematorium III (which was not torched in the rebellion). Buried and forgotten, these "Auschwitz Scrolls," lay waiting and unread for thirty-six years, until in 1980—nine years after their author's death—a worker investigating the defunct Birkenau site, discovered the buried thermos. These pages were also not Nadjari's only efforts at recording his thoughts and observations. He started a journal after the war and kept it until his death. This, also, was not revealed until after his death. Clearly, he never intended any of his writing for publication. Nevertheless, history is richer for his efforts. Nadjari resisted merely by surviving the war; he resisted by planning and participating in a rebellion on October 7, 1944, and he resisted by recording his thoughts and observations, which were evidence of the Nazi crimes. How different, in time and place, are the Scrolls of Auschwitz from the Dead Sea Scrolls, and yet, how similar.

The discovery of the Auschwitz Scrolls changed the narrative of Jewish resistance during the Holocaust in the same way that the Dead Sea Scrolls changed the narrative of Jewish life in the ancient world. Specifically, the Scrolls of Auschwitz provide evidence of resistance that Hannah Arendt denied existed. Like the Dead Sea Scrolls, which were disparate texts written by many different authors, it is known that many other Jews at Auschwitz buried their own documents during the Holocaust. After the war, documents that were buried under the ashes and bones in the crematoria were found. Among them were writings and documentation by Rabbi Leib Langfus. Rabbi Langfus's documents, which were found in 1945, 1952, and 1962, show us the need for a systematic search. Langfus's collections included images of the events in the camp, and his writings on life in Belzec Lab, the first camp designed to kill prisoners in an industrial manner. He wrote that he buried "various boxes and jars in the courtyard of Crematorium 2," and another "lies among bones strewn on the south-west side of the same courtyard." A third Scroll "lies in a pit of bones at Crematorium 1."[8] In total, eight documents by five authors were found: Zalman Gradowski, Zalman Lewental (1961), Chaim Herman, Rabbi Leib Langfus, and Marcel Nadjari. Zalman Gradowski, one of the authors of the eight documents, wrote "Dear

Scroll of Auschwitz from M. Nadjari. (Courtesy of the Resistance Project 2021)

Finder—search all the ground" presumably because he and others buried numerous documents around the crematoria where they worked.[9] Lewental wrote: "We will continue to do our part, we [will attempt] everything . . . to hide in the ground. He too mentions: "then you will find more—of the court-yard under the crem[atorium] . . . you will find many[10]—because we must up to now—events—in a chronological historic manner, to expose everything to the world. From now on we will bury everything in the earth." Gradowski's documents survive because Shlomo Dragon dug them up in March 1945, but also because they had been placed inside an aluminum canteen and buried in the ashes in the crematorium.

WARSAW GHETTO, RETURN TO NO. 18 MILA STREET, AND A REMARKABLE DISCOVERY

Perhaps the most famous armed and organized moment of Jewish Resistance during the war was the Warsaw Ghetto Uprising. The most famous site of the Warsaw Ghetto Uprising is the command bunker, originally a fortified smugglers' den, below a building at no. 18 Mila Street. There are entire books about the Mila 18 bunker and its place in history. It was in this bunker, in April and May 1943, that the leadership of the organized Jewish resistance movement—Mordechai Anielewicz, his girlfriend, Mira Fuchrer, and a ragtag group of Jewish fighters, all in their twenties—held off the greatest superpower army in the world in the last days of the Warsaw uprising. In the summer of 1942, three hundred thousand Jews were in the Warsaw Ghetto, and were murdered, or deported to labor camps before being sent to the death camps. SS units sent more than two hundred fifty thousand others to the Treblinka death camp. The last fifty thousand or so Jews left in the Ghetto knew that deportation and death were inevitable. In response, the Jewish underground movement mobilized, determined to resist the German effort to deport the remaining Ghetto residents, most of whom were by then in hiding. In April 1943, as Passover was to begin, the Germans prepared to liquidate the Ghetto. This initiated the uprising. Armed with pistols, home-made grenades, and a meager number of automatic weapons, the fighters understood the futility of their effort, but they were determined both to stop the deportations as well as decide the time and circumstances of their own deaths. They held out for a few days, until the Germans found and killed Anielewicz and captured the Mila 18 bunker. Amazingly, there were survivors. A group of six fighters, including Tosia Altman, who had managed to breathe through a concealed opening in the bunker, and they were found that night by Zivia Lubetkin and Marek Edelman, who helped the group escape from the ghetto via the sewers.[11] Our project was to find out how and where they escaped. By scanning with ERT the entire massive bunker we were able to locate the connection in the sewer that allowed some to get out. There were others who were heading for the same connector and were headed toward the Mila 18 bunker even as it was being gassed by the Nazis. The quote is a haunting memory of Masada, but it also shows us the insights that motivated these young Jews in Warsaw.

"It was the death sentence for one hundred and twenty Jewish fighters. It was not a quick death, either. The Germans used only enough gas to suffocate them slowly. Aryeh Vilner was the first to challenge: 'Let us kill ourselves rather than surrender to the Germans alive!'[12] The sound of shots filled the air. The Jewish fighters began taking their own lives. If a pistol didn't fire, its confused and wretched owner would beg a comrade to have pity and shoot him, but no one dared. Berl Broyde, who had been wounded in the hand and was unable to hold a gun, implored his comrades to end his life. Mordecai Anielewicz, who believed that water would remove the lethal effects of the gas, suggested they drench their faces. Someone suddenly discovered a way out of the bunker hidden from the Germans' view. Only a few managed to escape. The others died a slow death of poisoned suffocation. Thus perished the heroic flower of Jewish Warsaw. Jewish fighters found their deaths here, amongst them Mordecai Anielewicz, their handsome and courageous leader, a smile curled on the corner of his lips even during the final terror-filled hours."

We did a geophysical survey scan of the entire site in 2019 as part of the Geoscientists without Borders grant. It is helpful, sometimes necessary, to scan even well-trod sites to provide further physical evidence. Our scan revealed a whole world of evidence, including a piece missed by prior investigations, the escape route through the sewers of Warsaw. The sewers of Warsaw are centuries old; they are big, medieval passageways, not modern pipes. Our 2019 work traced the sewers to the presumed location of the bunker. On our return to Warsaw in 2021, we made an even more spectacular find. The actual bunker still exists, sealed off by time and urban development, under the streets and foundations of modern Warsaw. Fortunately for our studies and for history, this part of Warsaw was hardly developed in the decades after the war compared to the rest of the city. A large park and memorial to the Uprising was built over the general area, unwittingly preserving the bunker below. Using up-to-date geophysical methods, we were able to map the extent of the bunker without digging. The bunker complex is very large. It was understood to have been developed beneath three properties, numbers 16, 18, and 20, of the former Mila Street, and likely extended under the interior courtyards of those buildings to properties on the south side of the former Muranowska Street.

Our estimation is that it could comfortably accommodate more than 180 people. The 2021 investigation supplemented geophysical surveys completed at the site in July 2019.[13] We recommended to Polish authorities that they excavate immediately to rescue whatever remains of the bunker and its contents.

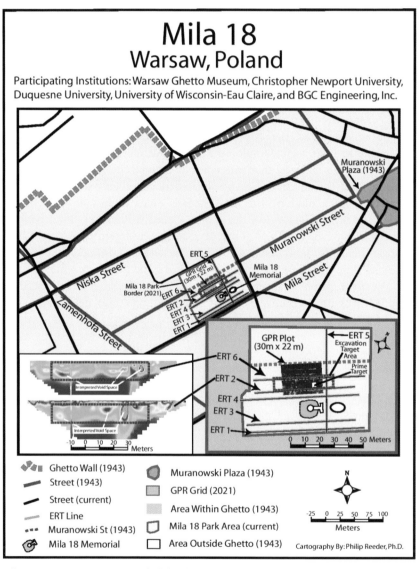

Mila 18 ERT scan. (Courtesy of Richard A. Freund, the Resistance Project 2021)

THE ESCAPE FROM FORT IX, KAUNAS, LITHUANIA

On Christmas Day, 1943, sixty-four Jewish prisoners escaped Fort IX, Kaunas, Lithuania. I have already written about Fort IX and the massacres that occurred there in my book *Archaeology of the Holocaust*. I returned with geophysicist Paul Bauman in July 2021 to study the escape. For three days, from July 23 to July 25, we reconstructed the exact timeline and route of the miraculous escape. We know a great deal about this event because the mastermind, Alex Faitelson, along with almost everyone who followed him, survived the war and wrote a memoir. This escape is significant not only for its success, but because news of it directly influenced the escape from Ponar that occurred in April 1944. We have testimony that some of the newspapers that were used for kindling for the burning brigade contained the story in late December and early January as the Nazis attempted to round up the escapees of Fort IX. Thus unintentionally the Fort IX escape may have initiated a series of steps toward the creation of the escape tunnel at Ponar that began in late January 1944.

It is thought that the prisoners, the "corpse-burners" or "burning brigade," had a plan for digging an escape tunnel that they began in November 1943. They found an area to dig and even an area to store the sand they excavated, but the length the tunnel would need to be and the foundations of the fort made completing the project impossible. As an alternative escape plan, the prisoners proposed making a key to open one of the empty, unused storerooms above the underground cell in which the group was locked at night. From this storeroom, a door opened to a passageway that led to the courtyard of the Fort. From the courtyard, the group could reach the outer wall of the fort. Even if the group managed to counterfeit a key to their cell, this plan required getting through the locked steel door that led to the passageway, and then getting over the wall. Their situation was so desperate, they resolved to try it.

To scale the wall, Paul Bauman explained, "there is the well-known rope ladder that [the prisoners] hung from the top of the wall [which is] found in the Museum at Fort IX. However, they also had a rigid, three piece, 6-meter-long wooden ladder"[14] that allowed them to scale the interior side of the wall. Alex Faitelson describes in *The Escape from IX Fort* that he had carpenters Boris Shtulman, from Moldavia, and Mendl Chas from the Kovno Ghetto, build "a six-meter long ladder made up of three sections of two meters each."[15] Faitelson notes that "the three-sectioned ladder was ready [on December 18] in the carpentry shop. The prisoners who had been let into the secret, prepared a rope ladder from army puttees [these likely would be military leg wrappings to protect from the cold]. All these items were stored

Fort IX escape sign. (Courtesy of Alastair McClymont, the Resistance Project, 2021)

in our cell and hidden under the bunks." He further explained that two ladders would have cut the escape time in half as well, of course."[16]

For the prisoners, the biggest obstacle was escaping to the courtyard of the fort. They had to break through the steel door that led from the storeroom to the passageway. A key was prepared, and the unused storeroom above their quarters was opened. Every day when the group was mustered to perform their duties of burning the corpses of the murdered Jews, two men of the group remained behind, claiming to be ill. According to camp rules, only two of the group were allowed to be ill and absent at any one time. One of them equipped with a penknife that had been found in the rotting clothes of a corpse and with a small hand-drill removed from a workshop, drilled through the heavy steel door, while the other kept watch. Gradually they made holes through the door and sawed through the steel between the holes. They also worked in the evenings, while the rest of the group sang songs and joked at the top of their voices to cover the sound of drilling. When not drilling, they would conceal the door behind a pile of rags. After weeks of strenuous labor, the hole in the steel door was finally made. It was thirty to forty centimeters, which was just enough for a person to pass through. The day for the flight was finally fixed for December 25, 1943—Christmas day.

Most preparations were completed, and partial rehearsals were begun. The tunnels through which the escaping prisoners had to pass were still blocked with wooden beams that had to be removed. As cover to remove the wood beams, they complained to their guards that the wood they received for the corpse burning pyres was wet and would not burn. They, therefore asked permission to take dry wood from the tunnels. The fort commandant suspected nothing and gave permission, and so the last obstacle was eliminated.

Tensions were extremely high. Everyone knew that, were the fort guards to discover any piece of the plan, they would put an end to the entire plan, and might very well murder all sixty-four members of the group as punishment. In fact, the extreme fear of death was always hanging over the group. The "burning brigade" might at any moment be killed and replaced by other prisoners. It was always at the whim of the camp commandant, and it had happened before. According to Faitelson, Christmas Eve was a half day of work. SS Captain Gratt addressed the sixty-four prisoners, and expressed his satisfaction for the pace of burning the bodies. He gave them alcohol and cigarettes in honor of the holiday. Gratt told them that they would not work for the two days of Christmas so they would rest properly, and return to work the on the following Monday with renewed strength. Furthermore, the Nazis assured the Jewish prisoners that they would not be killed at the end of their work. It was not inconceivable that this was a lie intended to raise morale, but the prisoners did not intend to find out. They were to put their escape plan into action that evening. The Jews gave the drink and tobacco to the guards as a bribe and distraction.

According to Faitelson, it was routine for the guards to lock the cell at 7 p.m. every night, and to turn off the lights and depart the building half an hour after that. The prisoners would then usually not be disturbed again until 5 a.m. the next morning. By 7 p.m. Christmas Eve, the workers were all in their cells, impatiently awaiting the arrival of the guards who would lock them in and then leave. During those hours of darkness, the prisoners hoped to carry out their plan. By 7 p.m., however, the guards had not arrived. They did not lock the workers in or put the lights out. Nobody understood what had happened—all feared the worst. A full hour passed in tense expectation. Then, at 8 p.m., two guards appeared and locked the doors. It turned out that in honor of Christmas they had wanted to give the Jewish prisoners an extra hour of time to themselves. Half an hour later, the lights were put out as usual and the guards left the building. The prisoners waited a little longer and then began carrying out their plan.

The final instructions were given. Any breach of discipline would endanger everyone, so the group was prepared to kill those who created a disturbance of the plan. Using the counterfeit key, they opened their cell and moved to the storeroom in absolute silence. The corridor floor and the iron stairs of the abandoned storeroom were covered with blankets to deaden any noise of their movements. They opened the storeroom with a key and reached the entry through the steel door. Without a word they all passed as planned through the hole and entered the passageway. They emerged into the courtyard, crossed a moat, and entered a second tunnel, which led them to the exterior wall of the fort, fortuitously, to a part obscured from the watchtowers., Faitelson writes, "At the foot of the six-meter high wall we attached the three-part ladder, tying it with army bandages. I go up the ladder and with a pincer which I took on the last day from Hauptstrumfuhrer Rudolf Radif Adler, I cut the barbed wire on top for the wall and attach the rope ladder made of army bandages to the wall posts. I take Heman Rubinfeld with me and return to the fort to get the rest of the prisoners out of the building."[17]

DISSIMULATION: HIDING AND HIDING IN PLAIN SIGHT

We know that many people hid from the Nazis. The courage and discipline necessary to hide in an attic, as Anne Frank did, is unimaginable to me. We all know that story as the archetype of the hidden child. Anne Frank's fate is known to the world. Her hiding place was eventually betrayed in Amsterdam and she died in Bergen-Belsen concentration camp. Hiding is one of the most psychologically traumatizing experiences for children. I worked on a project about an adolescent, Matilda Olkin, whose diary had been found in a local church in Panemunelis, Lithuania. It was a geoscience search for her remains and those of her family, who had been killed together in a nearby forest. For a while during the war, she and her family had hidden in the barn of the local church, but the family eventually refused to put the minister in harm's way any longer and turned themselves in to the local Nazi collaborators. They were taken to the forest and killed. In this case, I knew about the family from the diary and poetry of Matilda Olkin. The local priest hid her diary and poetry under the church's altar, again at the risk of his own life.

Perhaps most impressive to me are accounts of hiding in plain sight. One of the more fascinating instances of hiding occurred with the *Kashariyot*, or "Jewish women messenger/couriers," who risked their lives and provided an invaluable information conduit during the Holocaust by adopting the identity of non-Jewish women. Thus, they hid in plain sight; living out in the open as people they were not. The word *courier* does not do these women justice. These women did not just carry messages. They carried forged documents, cash for payments, guns and ammunition, and underground newspapers that gave the Jews of the Ghetto the news of what really was going on in the war and in other ghettoes. Their "hiding of their own identities" and the hiding of others identities made these women a link among various Jewish groups and to the outside world.

Hiding in a Variety of Contexts

From 1999 to 2000, I had worked on the story of Tivadar Soros, the father of George and Paul Soros, that one of my colleagues, Humphrey Tonkin, professor and president emeritus of the University of Hartford, had translated. The text was originally written by Tivadar in Esperanto. Esperanto is not a natural language, but an artificial one. It is "Yiddish" for everyone, a linguistic catch-all for the world. It was invented by a Jew, Ludwik Lejzer Zamenhof, from Bialystok and Warsaw (by way of Kaunas) and was supposed to make all of the divisive and different national languages of the world meaningless. Zamenhof intended Esperanto to enable all people to speak one language and thus would do away with the nationalism of national languages. Soros believed in that objective, and he chose to write his diary in Esperanto to further that cause. Soros wrote mostly in New York, two decades after the events of the war, as Tivadar himself was between speaking his native language and the language that he thought would save the world from the horrors of war and divisiveness. The book is entitled *Maskerado* ["masquerade" in Esperanto],[18] and it speaks to the most difficult form of Jewish resistance: attempting to not be identified as a Jew. In the book Tivadar decided to hide his whole family "in plain sight" in Budapest with forged documents. Because of their courage, Soros and his family survived the war.

While writing *Archaeology of the Holocaust* I included a section on the story of one of my neighbors, Florence Post. She has since passed away, but she is one of the reasons why I decided to work on a series of projects in Kovno, which is now the Lithuanian city of Kaunas. When I met her the first time she made me read the chapter in Alex Faitelson's *The Truth and Nothing but the Truth: Jewish Resistance in Lithuania* about her father. It was a short chapter, but it made a huge impact on me.[19] Since Alex Faitelson was the leader of the escape from IX Fort, I started thinking that this must be a similar story. It wasn't. Itzhak Nemenchik escaped from the extermination site of VII Fort, came back to the family in the Kovno Ghetto, and sent them all into hiding. Florence was sent to a farm where she was to pose as a child of a Polish family. She immediately had to stop speaking Yiddish and pretend to be a Polish farm girl. She recalled that often the local Lithuanians who collaborated with the Nazis during the war would just flash a look at her and she was sent into a deep terror. She lived to be an old woman because of her father's courage to divide up his family, fully aware that they might never meet again, so that perhaps someone would survive the war. Nemenchik's courage and sacrifice were yet another example of resistance against the Nazis. I was moved as I read about his story, because it provided details that, in my experience, no other survivor testimony had. She was a hidden child during the Holocaust, and thanks to the courage of her parents and her own, she and her family survived. Accounts of hiding in the midst of a local population is often not seen as Jewish resistance. In my thinking the amount of courage necessary to hide in the midst of a potentially hostile local population is an extreme form of Jewish resistance. It is, to be sure, a risk to the righteous gentiles who housed them, but it was a form of resistance for the Jews who agreed to hide as well.

The largest group of hidden Jewish resistance fighters were the children. Children were continually at risk during the Holocaust. Many were saved by being placed in hiding, but the psychological toll on these children was tremendous. Some were never able to come to grips with the abandonment, even though it led directly to their surviving the Holocaust. It was not uncommon among those rare cases where parent and child survived the Holocaust separately for the child not to recognize the parent when reunited. For decades after the war, these survivors lived alone with their trauma, for it was not until the 1990s that organizations such as the Hidden Child Foundation had the means and the will to unite this community and define their suffering. One event in New York City attracted over sixteen hundred survivors. It was a watershed event for these children, now adults, who did not know how to classify themselves. Finally, they could tell their stories to others who had the same experiences.

In 2020, I received a call from a woman in West Hartford, Connecticut. I listened to her for an hour as she told me the story of her own hidden childhood in the Holocaust. It was incredibly moving. She really had not even told her own children the full story of her escape from the Vilna Ghetto just days before the entire Ghetto was liquidated. It was an unexpected honor that she chose to open up to me. She was born in the Vilna Ghetto in late March 1942. Her uncle, a leather producer, had a work permit, and could leave the Ghetto daily to serve the Nazis with his trade. When she was seventeen months old, her uncle wrapped her in his leather goods and left for an appointment with a client. He dropped the baby off with a farmer near Vilnius. She lived with him and his son and his mother until 1947, when her mother came back to retrieve her. It was an emotionally wrenching experience, as the only family that she ever really knew was not really hers, and suddenly she was meeting her biological mother. Her biological family took her and later emigrated to the United States. She was educated in Brooklyn and not allowed to have contact with her adoptive father until she was seventeen years old. In an exchange of letters, she learned of the love and compassion that this man had for her, and how his efforts had saved her life. Listening to her story I was reminded of the testimonies of other Jewish resistance fighters throughout the Holocaust that I had encountered, people whose names are written about in the annals of Jewish resistance. I could hear the voices of Matilda Olkin of Rokiskis, of Selma Engel and Esther Raab from Sobibor, of Zevia Lubetkin from the Warsaw Ghetto, and of Florence Post. They were children who had become resistance fighters through circumstances beyond their control. This woman had a letter that she shared with me. It was the last letter she had received from her rescuer and adoptive father. He had suffered badly after the war under the Soviets. She had been able to send him precious small items of food and clothing that helped him in the dark days of the 1960s and 1970s. In the letter, he wrote: "First I saved you and now you have saved me." Stories such as these allow us to see the Jews of the Holocaust era as real individuals, rather than eternal victims.

SEARCHING FOR SPIRITUAL RESISTANCE IN RIGA

Testimonies suggest that as many as six hundred prayer areas were constructed in the Warsaw Ghetto despite the fact that the Nazis officially banned prayer services. There was a synagogue, probably better described as a prayer room, at HKP 562 labor camp. Religious literature produced and sermons given by Rabbi Kalonymous Kalman Shapira are preserved in the Ringelblum Archives of the Warsaw Ghetto. Kaunas Rabbi Ephraim Oshry wrote *Min HaMaamakim* (From the Depths). All of this is evidence of religious or spiritual resistance.

Rabbi Joseph Hirsch Carlebach was the Orthodox chief rabbi of Hamburg who had served Germany in World War I and was a natural scientist by training. In early December 1941, nearly four thousand Jews from Austria and Germany were sent to the Jungfernhof camp outside Riga, Latvia; Rabbi Carlebach among them. These German and Austrian Jews had nothing in common with the local population and no way to communicate with them. Jungfernhof was not a labor camp or an extermination camp. It was not even a camp with barbed wire fences. The camp was barracks and latrines, used as overflow housing for thousands of German-speaking Jews intended for other camps on the Eastern Front. December 14, 1941, shortly after their arrival, the holiday of Hanukkah began. The Hanukkah celebration found Rabbi Carlebach lighting candles for the multitudes in what was hopefully an inspiring moment in freezing, horrible barracks. Rabbi Carlebach's job in the camp was to teach the children, and he was offered slightly better accommodation than the common prisoners. But he chose to live in the barracks. He knew he needed to be with his people, and continued to pray during his stay. Daily he would see people in his "office" at the hospital and give spiritual comfort and prayer. He carried with him his prayer implements and matzah that he had helped bake. He found a way to bury his own brother properly; he had died in the early days at Jungfernhof. The term *Hesed Shel Emet*, which in Hebrew means "a true act of kindness," describes the Rabbi's actions. On March 26, 1942, he and others were marched into Bikernieki forest and shot by the SS.

I know of Rabbi Carlebach's story from his son, Shlomo, who survived the war and still lives in New York. He gave a USC Shoah Foundation testimony in 1997. I had studied his story when I arrived at Jungfernhof to search for the mass burial site. We were looking for the bodies of approximately eight hundred Jews who died during the early winter months of 1942. We needed to locate the mass grave in a field with little sign of any disturbance. We knew that the area was used for farming, so the upper layers of the field showed wear and tear, but the actual mass grave needed to be a very specific deep cut in the earth. (Photogrammetry of the whole field did aid us by showing micro-topographies in the field that were different.) Again, a witness testimony provided the important clue. Richard Yashek's book, *The Story of My Life*, gave detailed information about the circumstances of the digging of the mass grave:

> By May [1942], the ground had sufficiently thawed so that two mass graves could be dug over a period of days to bury 800 or so bodies that had accumulated since December of the previous year. The mounds eventually reached six to eight feet in height. During the remaining months of 1942, these mounds began to discharge foul smelling gases from the decomposing bodies and continued to smell and shrink. Eventually, where there had been a mound several meters high, gradually became a depression of two feet or so in each of the pits. So we were constantly reminded that hundreds of people lay buried here, with no identity, no markers, no remembrances of their former beings. In time, as the settlement of the mounds slowed, we were able to add fresh soil to level the area.[20]

The account ends with a postscript saying that still in early June 1942 some other boys were sent into the field with other children (there may have been thirty to forty, aged twelve to seventeen) shoveling, and distributing top soil on the grave. For our search, we used a noninvasive, subsurface method that includes multiple steps to create a picture of what lies below the surface. We know what happened from testimonies, historical photos, and other evidence, but we were working to pinpoint the site of the atrocities and could not dig indiscriminately, for fear of disturbing long-buried Jewish bodies. We were looking for two very closely aligned mass graves in the field.

Some of our results are shown in figure 4.10. The section marked in red along the line of the ERT shows two very distinct dug areas that line up side by side. The distinctive cuts and the two separate mounds are very prominent here. The middle section between the two is different from the two trench cuts. The trenches are four meters deep. These contain the bodies. They align as two separate and distinct mounds that are under a covering of topsoil. In order to confirm the trench, we then did a very detailed Ground Penetrating Radar grid on top of the area. It reveals the details of the ERT and again shows how there are two distinctive trenches with an area in between the two. The amazing testimony and the findings of our geoscience in the same field eighty years later speak volumes about what this type of work can do to preserve Holocaust history and places. It is rare to find testimonies of an unknown site and then do the work and discover just how exact their descriptions match the science.

Map of Jungfernhof camp, Latvia. (Courtesy of Philip Reeder, the Resistance Project 2021)

CULTURAL, LITERARY, MUSICAL, AND ARTISTIC RESISTANCE DURING THE HOLOCAUST

In his book *The Book Smugglers,* Dr. David Fishman writes about the Jews of the Vilna Ghetto who risked their lives to save books of significant Jewish cultural value and relevance.[21] The Nazis planned to destroy almost everything of Jewish culture, but they intended to keep a few choice items for display in their Museum of Destroyed Peoples. The Jews conscripted to select the items for exhibition therefore had access to books they could smuggle to safety. These Jews became known as the *Book Smugglers.* Perhaps it is difficult to imagine the value placed on written works simply because they were written works and not because they were fashioned from precious metals or had bejeweled covers. Today, when almost all information is beamed electronically to hand-held devices and bookstores are disappearing for want of customers, I find it difficult to convince my young students that people risked their lives to save books, and not books of great material value, but of great spiritual and cultural value. As an example of the kind of book that was saved, I show them one that came from the same place where we had been working for the past five years: the Great Synagogue and Shulhoyf of Vilna. It is not a prayer book or Torah scroll, although some of the saved documents were. It is a simple registry of the affairs of the Gaon of Vilna's Kloyz (prayer house) that started with a signature of the son of the eighteenth-century Vilna Gaon. The book was saved from destruction by the renown poet Avraham Sutzkever, who also signed it, and wrote about his own journey to save the book at the risk of his own life while interred in the Vilnius Ghetto in 1944. It is because a great poet like Sutzkever risked his life daily to save books like this that I know that cultural Jewish resistance occurred not only in the Holocaust but also in historical Judaism.

While speaking with Dr. Fishman at the Great Synagogue of Vilna in summer 2021, he reminded me how difficult it is today to appreciate the risks that artists, musicians, poets, and writers faced in continuing to resist the Nazis by teaching and writing. Yet many works of art were produced in the Ghettos and camps during the war. The musical works that serve as Jewish resistance include children's operas such as the one that my own university featured in 2021, *Brundibár. Brundibár* was composed by Jewish Czech composer Hans Krása with a libretto by Adolf Hoffmeister, in 1938 for a competition, and rehearsals started in 1941 at the Jewish orphanage in Prague, which served as a temporary educational facility for Jewish children separated from their parents by the war. It premiered in Theresienstadt, a model concentration camp, which the Nazis set up to show the Red Cross that the reports about extermination camps were not true. The production was directed by Zelenka Rosenbaum and choreographed by Camilla Rosenbaum and was performed fifty-five times in the following year. *Brundibár* is one of those productions that will attract audiences of children and their parents and grandparents because it is not directly about the horrors of the Holocaust. It is a parable set in a small village and presents themes of working together to overcome adversity and the triumph of good over evil. The "mean organ grinder" (modeled after Hitler) is defeated by a group of children and the local animals. It is a fairy tale like Hansel and Gretel, and it allows us to drift back and forth between the atrocities of the Nazis and the world we live in today with challenges that call upon us to make decisions that require resistance.

IS THE PEN MIGHTIER THAN THE SWORD?

Abraham Tory of the Kovno Ghetto, and hundreds of others during the Holocaust, documented the crimes of the Nazis in their diaries. They worried that there were not going to be any Jews living after the Holocaust, and so their efforts were almost apocalyptic. They kept diaries and journals to tell their stories, drew illustrations of the places where they lived, and created maps of the places where they hid. The risky and often secret documentation projects were carried out in small and large cities like Bialystok, Vilna, and Lodz. Unlike the armed revolts, escapes, and testimonies, these detailed documentation projects had far-reaching implications after the war at the Nuremberg Trials and later in the trial of Eichmann in Jerusalem. To document the crimes of the Nazis in the Ghetto was as risky as smuggling weapons. Tory prepared five small wooden crates containing his own diary, the compilation of orders, the 1942 yearbook, the Ältestenrat office reports, art, and photographs in a bunker beneath Block C in the Kovno Ghetto. He escaped on March 23, 1944, spending the final months of the war in hiding on a farm outside Kovno. Yet it was the publication of his diary and the preservation of other secret archive documents that made the most durable impact. They indicted both Nazis and collaborators after the war. It was consulted by investigators as evidence against Lithuanian and German perpetrators since the 1960s. His diary is full of explicit detail, and he had extraordinary knowledge because of his role in the administration of the Ghetto. It was published in Hebrew in 1983 and in English five years later as *Surviving the Holocaust: The Kovno Ghetto Diary*.

THE SEARCH FOR ARCHIVES IN THE WARSAW GHETTO

It is quite possible that Josephus Flavius recorded his series of writings in the first century CE because he feared that the Jews would be destroyed, and there would be no record of the illustrious history of Jewish life and their contributions to society. The Dead Sea Scrolls were, it is supposed, hidden in caves because the Jews who placed them there feared that the ideas and texts of the Jews would not survive. The Jews in the Warsaw Ghetto were already afraid in 1941 that all Jews would be killed by the Nazis, and those in the Ghetto wanted to preserve what they could of Jewish culture. Dr. Emmanuel Ringelblum, a prisoner in the Ghetto and a well-known Jewish historian, formed a group called the *Oyneg Shabes*, or "the Joy of the Sabbath." In Jewish tradition, this is a joyful gathering following Sabbath prayers. This group, which included historians, writers, rabbis, and social workers, was dedicated to chronicling the life of the Jews of Poland in the Warsaw Ghetto. Emmanuel Ringelblum was not the Josephus of his period, but the Jews in the Ghetto had a knowledge of their history and a deeply ingrained notion that they needed to document the atrocities of their captors.

As many as sixty volunteers worked as a team, collecting the materials submitted for the archives, which included essays, diaries, drawings, wall posters, and other materials describing life and the Nazi atrocities in the Ghetto. The collection work started in September 1939 and ended in January 1943. The group knew of the coming liquidation of the Ghetto and of the planned uprising against the Nazis, and they feared the archives would be destroyed. To preserve what they could, they broke the archives into three different pieces, placed the separate collections into large metal milk jugs and buried the jugs in three different locations. All these measures were taken so that some of the documents might survive the impending destruction of the Ghetto and of Polish Jewry. The materials were hidden in 1942 and 1943 so that even if everyone was killed the documents might be found to tell the stories of the devastation. Soon after, the Warsaw Ghetto and most of Warsaw was completely destroyed by events of the war.

The first part of the Ringelblum archives was recovered in 1946 by a survivor of the uprising who knew its location. Despite the utter destruction of Warsaw in the intervening three years of war, he was able to use local points of reference to find one of the jugs. He was unable to locate the other two. The second part of the Ringelblum archives was found by accident near the first part of the archives in 1950 by a construction crew. The third part of the archives has always been assumed to have been buried in another location and must be where there had been heavy fighting. It remains hidden. It is known to exist; and it is mentioned by several testimonies of the survivors

A Ringelblum Archive Milk Can. (Courtesy of A. Richard Freund, the Resistance Project 2021)

of the Ringelblum group. Very few people were actually involved in hiding the archives, so the knowledge of where it was hidden has been lost. One of the places where it was thought to have been hidden was at the far end of the Ghetto where the brush makers' workshop was located. The area suffered massive destruction and the site was never definitively located until the summer of 2021.

UNESCO has named the Ringelblum Archives as containing some of the most significant artifacts in Polish history. Finding the third piece would be immeasurably important, but so would be any of the different archives that the Jews maintained inside of the Ghetto. We do have clues to its location. According to those who were a part of the group, the third part of the archives was placed at the brush maker's factory at Świętojerska Street, which was the scene of heavy fighting and destruction in 1943. Of course, nothing remains of the original structures; that part of Warsaw has been completely redeveloped several times over the past seventy-eight years. In fact, because of the level of destruction in this area, the entire area was redrawn, reconstructed, and renamed. Near the area the Embassy of the People's Republic of China stands at the corner of the now renamed streets. Needless to say, that has complicated the numerous past searches for the last piece of the archives. China granted permission for a major search and excavation in 2003 on the grounds of the embassy, but nothing was found. I was not part of that search, but the search was mentioned to me back in 2008 when I was in Warsaw for consultations on Sobibor. For over a decade we investigated the presumed location and found nothing. Then, on our visit in 2021, thanks to a Polish colleague, Dr. Jacek Konik, we discovered in the old city records that the streets and their names had changed completely. When Świętojerska Street was rebuilt after the war, the original path of the street was not preserved. The new street was rebuilt along a slightly different course that put the brush makers' workshop in Krasinski Park across the street from the embassy. Obviously, buildings we thought should be in one place, relative to the street, would now be somewhere else. This was my "Indiana Jones-Raiders of the Lost Ark" moment. I realized that we, and all the other searchers, had been digging in the wrong place!

Krasinski Park was not part of the Chinese Embassy, which simplified the search preparations immensely. Still, we could not simply dig up a large city park. Our geoscience and archaeology group suggested to the Warsaw Ghetto Museum that, since the artifacts were buried in metal containers, and since our geoscience technologies were geared to find subsurface artifacts, especially metal, without excavation, we could use these technologies to identify a site for excavation in the park. In concert with the Warsaw Ghetto Museum, we mapped the portion of the park where the old Świętojerska

Map of Krasinski Park. (Courtesy of Philip Reeder, the Resistance Project 2021)

Street would have run in the period of the Warsaw Ghetto, and we surveyed the boundaries of the brush factory. Furthermore, we mapped what appeared to be a buried wall segment with a large metal object buried beneath that. We surveyed 220 meters, and many of the areas contained metal, walls, and artifacts. When we left in the summer of 2021 we had not yet begun a physical excavation, but this metal object may very well be part of the Ringelblum archives, the Bund archives (or any other archives of the community), and most probably a series of other community records. In late October, 2021 our local Polish archaeologist, Jacek Konik, from the Warsaw Ghetto Museum was able to get a permit for excavations in a small area with metal signatures in the park. In the excavations we found parts of a community archives that indeed did have a major metal signature in the center of the excavations. It was the metal beam from the ceiling of the building.

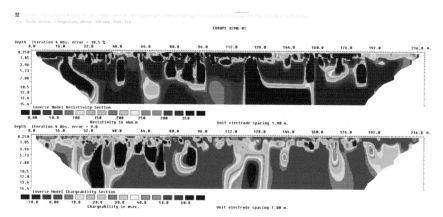

Multiple sites for buried archives in ERT scan. (Courtesy of Paul Bauman, the Resistance Project 2021)

In the work we did in the summer of 2021, we surveyed over 120 meters in the park and many other metal deposits were found. It is what makes geoscience and archaeology so exciting. We have multiple targets, and we know exactly where we want to excavate when the opportunity arrives.

Notes

CHAPTER 1

1. Plato, *Critias*, trans. Benjamin Jowett, accessed June 23, 2020, http://www.clas sicallibrary.org/plato/dialogues/18_critias.htm.

2. A. Rodriguez-Ramirez et al., "The Role of Neo-tectonics in the Sedimentary Infilling and Geomorphological Evolution of the Guadalquivir Estuary (Gulf of Cadiz, SW Spain) during the Holocene" *Geomorphology* 219, no. 15 (August 2014): 126–40, and endnote 4.

3. Josephus Flavius, *Antiquities of the Jews*, 8.3.7.

4. Antonio Rodríguez-Ramírez, José Noel Pérez-Asensio b, Ana Santos a, Gonzalo Jiménez-Moreno, Juan J.R. Villarías-Robles, Eduardo Mayoral, Sebastián Celestino-Pérez, Enrique Cerrillo-Cuenca, José Antonio López-Sáez , Ángel Leóng, Carmen Contreras, "Atlantic Extreme Wave Events during the Last Four Millennia in the Guadalquivir Estuary, SW Spain," *Quaternary Research* 83 (2015): 24–40.

CHAPTER 3

1. In 1948, famed archaeologist and leading biblical scholar William Albright made the extraordinary claim that the Dead Sea Scrolls were "the greatest archaeological find of the 20th century." https://www.foxnews.com/opinion/why-an-incredible -new-discovery-proves-that-the-dead-sea-scrolls-belong-to-israel accessed on April 24, 2022. Peter Flint, The Dead Sea Scrolls: The Greatest Archaeological Discovery of Our Time, https://www.khouse.org/articles/2011/960/print/, accessed April 24, 2022.

2. Josephus Flavius, *The Wars of Jews*, VII 8.6, translated by William Whiston. In *Josephus: Complete Works* (Grand Rapids: Kregel Publications, 1978), 601.

3. William Claiborne, "Rights for Ancient Bones Stir Israeli Dispute," *Washington Post*, May 7, 1982, https://www.washingtonpost.com/archive/politics/1982/05/07/rites-for-ancient-bones-stir-israeli-dispute/087e7a6a-b2fc-466e-8fe2-46398dc0c9ab/, accessed on September 12, 2021.

4. Y. Aharoni, "The Expedition to the Judean Desert, 1960, Expedition B," *Israel Exploration Journal* 11, nos. 1–2 (1961): 11–24, Pls. 4–11C; Y. Aharoni, "The Expedition to the Judean Desert, 1961, Expedition B—The Cave of Horror," *Israel Exploration Journal* 12, nos. 3–4 (1962): 186–99, Pls. 23–34; Y. Aharoni and B. Rottenberg, *In the Footsteps of Kings and Rebels* (Jerusalem: Masada, 1960).

5. Alan J. Witten, *Handbook of Geophysics and Archaeology* (London: Equinox, London), 317.

6. Yigael Yadin, *The Message of the Scrolls* (New York: Simon & Schuster, 1957), 14.

7. Theodore Heline, *The Dead Sea Scrolls* (Santa Monica, CA: New Age Bible and Philosophy, 1957).

8. Charles Francis Potter, *The Lost Years of Jesus Revealed* (New York: Fawcett Publications, 1959).

9. O. Preston Robinson, *The Dead Sea Scrolls and Original Christianity* (Salt Lake City, UT: Deseret Book Company, 1958).

10. Yadin, *The Message of the Scrolls*, 14.

11. Yadin, 14.

12. Will Varner, "What Is the Importance of the Dead Sea Scrolls?" Christian-Answers.Net, https://christiananswers.net/q-abr/abr-a023.html, accessed on April 24, 2022.

13. Nelson Glueck, "Out of Yesterday, a Symbol for Today," *New York Times*, May 11, 1958, 6.

14. This version is from Harry Orlinsky, "The Mysterious Mr. Green," *Reform Judaism* 20, no. 3 (Spring 1992): 47–48.

15. Andre Dupont-Sommer, *The Dead Sea Scrolls: A Preliminary Survey* (Oxford: Blackwell, 1952).

16. "Christianity Jesus Christ and the Essenes: Similarities and Differences," Ask Why!, http://www.askwhy.co.uk/christianity/0180JesusEssene.php, accessed on April 24, 2022.

17. David B. Smith, "I Had a Dream," Ezine Articles, http://ezinearticles.com/?I-Had-A-Dream---A-Sermon-On-Acts-11&id=533143

18. Edmund Wilson, "The Scrolls from the Dead Sea," *New Yorker*, May 14, 1955.

19. Richard Freund, "How the Dead Sea Scrolls Influenced Reform Judaism," *Journal of the American Jewish Archives*, 61, no. 1 (Spring 2009): 115–43. All references to individual sermons that are now archived at the Hebrew Union College in Cincinnati can be found in my article "The Dead Sea Scrolls, Hebrew Union College and Reform Judaism 1948–2008," in *The Dead Sea Scrolls and Contemporary Culture: Proceedings of the International Conference held at the Israel Museum, Jerusalem (July 6–8, 2008)*, edited by Adolfo Roitman, Lawrence H. Schiffman, and Shani Tzoref (Leiden: Brill, 2011), 621–47.

20. Nelson Glueck, "New Light on the Dim Past," *New York Times*, November 20, 1955.

21. See "In Memory of Reb Zalman Schachter-Shalomi—Once the B'nai Or Rebbe, Always a Radical Teacher," Notes from a Jewish Thoreau (blog), http://rooster613.blogspot.com/2014/07/in-memory-of-reb-zalman-schachter.html, accessed on April 24, 2022.

22. Cyrus Gordon, "The Dead Sea Scrolls" *Reconstructionist*, 22, no. 6 (May 4, 1956): 14.

23. "Dead Sea Scrolls Editor's Exit Tied to Anti-Semitic Remarks," December 12, 1990, AP News, https://apnews.com/article/3532cf8776a8970b9039ec370c2f f4b6, accessed on April 24, 2022, "Ouster of an Anti-Judaist: Scandal engulfs the chief Dead Sea Scrolls editor, *Time*, January 14, 1991, https://content.time.com/time /subscriber/article/0,33009,972124,00.html, accessed on April 24, 2022.

24. Tzvi Zahavy, "My Postmodern Review of Three Jewish," Talmud, 2006, http://tzvee.blogspot.com/2006/aa/my-postmodern-review-of-three-Jewish.html (accessed April 2009).

CHAPTER 4

1. Salo W. Baron, "Newer Emphases in Jewish History," *Jewish Social Studies* 25 no. 4 (1963): 245–58. Reprinted in Baron, *History and Jewish Historians: Essays and Addresses* (Philadelphia: Jewish Publication Society, 1964), 90–106.

2. Quoted in Yigael Yadin, *Masada: Herod's Fortress and the Zealots Last Stand* (Jerusalem: Steinmatzky, 1966), 97. The Works of Flavius Josephus / War of the Jews / Book 7.7. William Whiston, 1737 translation.

3. Ken Stanford, "The New Dead Sea Scroll Discovery at the Cave of Horror in Israel," World of the Bible, March 16, 2021, https://www.worldofthebible.com /the-new-dead-sea-scroll-discovery-at-horror-cave-in-israel/ (accessed September 12, 2021).

4. Yadin, *Masada*, 201.

5. Mordechai Aviam has noted various archaeological finds as particular Jewish ethnic or cultural markers. Among these he includes: (1) Galilean coarse ware (GCW); (2) Hasmonaen coins; (3) mikva'ot; (4) stone vessels; (5). Kefar Hannania ware, in particular the first-century CE "Galilean bowl"; (6) secondary burial in ossuaries; (7) secret caves/tunnels/hideaways; and (8) synagogues. Mordechai Aviam, "Distribution Maps of Archaeological Data in the Galilee as an Attempt to Create Ethnic and Religion Zones," in *Religion, Ethnicity, and Identity in Ancient Galilee: A Region in Transition*, ed. Jürgen Zangenberg, Harold W. Attridge, and Dale B. Martin (Tübingen, Germany: Mohr Siebeck, 2007), 115–32. I have added and collapsed many of these categories here.

6. Marcel Nadjary, "Marcel Nadjary Auschwitz Testimony," trans. the German-Canadian Centre for Innovation and Research, https://www.scribd.com/document

/361899530/Marcel-Nadjary-Auschwitz-testimony. Nadjary did write a Greek memoir that has not been translated into English: Marcel Nadjary, *Χρονικό 1941–1945*
[Chronicle 1941–1945] (Thessaloniki: Etz-Chaim Foundation, 1991).

7. Bernard Mark, *The Scrolls of Auschwitz*, trans. Sharon Neemani (Tel Aviv: Am
'Oved Pub. House, 1985).

8. Nicholas Chare and Dominic Williams, *Matters of Testimony: Interpreting the
Scrolls of Auschwitz* (London: Berghahn Books, 2016), 93.

9. Gideon Greif, *We Wept without Tears: Testimonies of the Jewish Sonderkommando from Auschwitz* (New Haven, CT: Yale University Press, 2005), 48.

10. Zalman Lewental, "Diary," in Mark, *The Scrolls of Auschwitz*, 221. Mark's work
included only four of the manuscripts discovered before his death in 1966. His wife
finished the work, and it was published in Tel Aviv in 1985. In 1971, the Auschwitz
State Museum published its own translation of the works and included an addition
one of Chaim Herman. In 1973, an additional manuscript attributed to Leib Langfus
was added.

11. Avinoam Patt, *The Jewish Heroes of Warsaw* (Detroit: Wayne State University
Press, 2021), 328–29. Quoted in "Revolt amid the Darkness," 206. Reprinted from
Zivia Lubetkin, *In the Days of Destruction and Revolt* (Israel: Ghetto Fighters' House,
1981), 178–246.

12. This is an example of how the Masada experience did influence the thinking
of Jews during the uprising. Y. Lamdan had written a poem in 1927 on the subject
["Masada: A Historical Epic"] that had become very well known by the young Warsaw Jewish rebels in the bunker.

13. They are detailed in a technical report available at https://seg.org/About
-SEG/Geoscientists-Without-Borders/Projects/detail/lithuania.

14. Correspondence from June 5, 2021.

15. Alex Faitelson, *The Escape from the IX Fort*, trans. Ethel Broido (Kaunas,
Lithuania: Spausdino Gabijos, 1998), 74.

16. Faitelson, 76.

17. Faitelson, 92.

18. Tivadar Soros, *Maskerado: Dancing around Death in Nazi Hungary* (Edinburgh:
Canongate Books, 2000).

19. Alex Faitelson, "The Fate of Itzhak Nemenchik," in *The Truth and Nothing but
the Truth: Jewish Resistance in Lithuania* (Jerusalem: Gefen 2006), 91–94.

20. Richard Yashek, *The Story of My Life* (Reading, PA: Self-published, 1996),
30–32.

21. David Fishman, *The Book Smugglers: Partisans, Poets, and the Race to Save Jewish Treasures from the Nazis* (Chicago: University of Chicago Press, 2017).

Bibliography

CHAPTER 1: THE ARCHAEOLOGY OF ATLANTIS

Balmuth, A. Gilman, and L. Prado-Torreira, eds. *Encounters and Transformations: The Archaeology of Iberia in Transition*. Monographs in Mediterranean Archaeology 7, Sheffield, UK: Sheffield Academic Press, 1997.

Berlitz, Charles. *Atlantis, The Eighth Continent*. New York: Putnam, 1984.

———. *The Mystery of Atlantis*. New York: Grosset & Dunlap, 1969.

Bramwell, James. *Lost Atlantis*. London: Cobden-Sanderson, 1937.

Brennan, Herbie. *The Atlantis Enigma*. London: Piatkus, 2000.

Byrom, James. *Lost Atlantis*. San Bernardino, CA: Borgo Press, 1980.

Castleden, Rodney. *Atlantis Destroyed*. New York: Routledge, 1998.

———. *Minoans: Life in Bronze Age Crete*. New York: Routledge, 1990.

Celestino, S., N. Rafel, and X-L. Armada. *Contacto cultural entre el Mediterráneo y el Atlántico* (siglos XII–VIII ane): La precolonización a debate (Serie Arqueológica 11). Madrid: Consejo Superior de Investigaciones Científicas (CSIC), 2008.

Celestino-Pérez, S., ed. *Cancho Roano VI* (The Sanctuary-Palace). Archaeological Series, Badajoz, Spain: Instituto de Arqueologia de Merida, CSIC, 1996.

———. *Cancho Roano, VIII: Los Materiales Arqueologicos*, Badajoz, Spain: Instituto de Arqueologia de Merida, CSIC 2003.

———. *Cancho Roano, IX*, Badajoz, Spain: Instituto de Arqueologia de Merida, CSIC 2003.

Celestino-Pérez, S. "Precolonization and Colonization in the Interior of Tartessos." In *Colonial Encounters in Ancient Iberia: Phoenician, Greek and Indigenous Relations*, edited by M. Dietler and C. Lopez-Ruiz, 229–51. Chicago: University of Chicago Press, 2009).

Chamorro, Javier G. "Survey of Archaeological Research on Tartessos." *American Journal of Archaeology* 91, no. 2 (April 1987), 197–232.

Chapin, H. *The Search for Atlantis*. New York: Crowell-Collier Press, 1968.

149

Collins, A. *Gateway to Atlantis: The Search for a Source of a Lost Civilization.* New York: Carroll and Graf, 2000.

Cross, F. M. "The Old Phoenician Inscription from Spain Dedicated to Hurrian Astarte." *Harvard Theological Review,* 64 (1971): 189–95.

de Boer, Jelle Zeilinga, and Donald Theodore Sanders. *Volcanoes in Human History: The Far-Reaching Effects of Major Eruptions.* Princeton, NJ: Princeton University Press, 2002.

De Camp, L. Sprague. *Lost Continents: The Atlantis Theme in History, Science, and Literature.* New York: Gnome Press, 1954.

Donnelly, I. *Atlantis: The Antediluvian World.* London: Sidgwick & Jackson, 1970.

Doumas, C. "The Minoan Eruption of the Santorini Volcano." *Antiquity* 48, no. 190 (1974): 110–15.

———. *Thera, Pompeii of the Ancient Aegean: Excavations at Akrotiri, 1967–79.* New York: Thames and Hudson, 1983.

Dunbavin, P. *Atlantis of the West: The Case for Britain's Drowned Megalithic Civilization.* New York: Carroll & Graf, 2003.

Ebon, M. *Atlantis: The New Evidence.* New York: New American Library, 1977.

Elat, M. "Tarshish and the Problem of the Phoenician Colonization in the Western Mediterranean." *Orientalia Lovaniensia Perodica* 13 (1982): 55–69.

Ellis, R. *Imagining Atlantis.* New York: Alfred A. Knopf, 1998.

Freund, R. *Digging through History: Archaeology and Religion from Atlantis to the Holocaust.* Lanham, MD: Rowman & Littlefield, 2012.

Gill, C. "The Genre of the Atlantis Story." *Classical Philology* 72, no. 4 (October 1977): 287–304.

Gomez Toscano, Francisco. "La ocupación protohistórica entre el Guadiana y el Guadalquivirdel mito a la realidad." *SPAL: Revista de Prehistoria y Arqueología* 11 (2002): 151–60.

González de Canales, Fernando, L. Serrano, and J. Llompart. "Las evidencias más antiguas de la presencia Fenicia en el sur de la Península 1. *Mainake* 28 (2006): 105–28.

Gutiérrez-Mas, J. M., C. Juan, and J. A. Morales. "Evidence of High-Energy Events in Shelly Layers Interbedded in Coastal Holocene Sands in Cadiz Bay (South-West Spain)." *Earth Surface Processes and Landforms* 34, no. 6 (2004): 810–23.

James, P. *The Sunken Kingdom: The Atlantis Mystery Solved.* London: Pimlico, 1996.

Joseph, F. *The Atlantis Encyclopedia.* Franklin Lakes, NJ: New Page Books, 2005.

———. *The Destruction of Atlantis.* Olympia Fields, IL: Atlantis Research Publishers, 1987.

Kühne, R. W. "A Location for 'Atlantis'?" *Antiquity* 78, no. 300 (2004).

Lipinski, E. "Tarshish." In *Theological Dictionary of the Old Testament, Vol. 15,* edited by G. J. Botterweck, H. Ringgren, and H.-J. Fabry, 790–93. Grand Rapids: Wm. B. Eerdmans, 2006.

Lopez-Saez, Jose, et al. "Mid-Late Holocene Environmental and Cultural Dynamics at the South-West Tip of Europe (Doñana National Park, SW Iberia, Spain)." *Journal of Archaeological Science: Reports* 22 (December 2018): 58–78.

Luce, J. V. *The End of Atlantis: New Light on an Old Legend.* New York: Thames and Hudson, 1969.

Manning, S. W. *A Test of Time: The Volcano of Thera and the Chronology and History of the East Mediterranean in the Mid Second Millennium BC.* Oxford, UK: Oxbow Books, 1999.

Marinatos, S. "The Volcanic Destruction of Minoan Crete." *Antiquity* 13 (1939): 425.

Pérez, S., and S. López-Ruiz. "New Light on the Warrior Stelae from Tartessos, *Antiquity* 80 (2006): 89–101.

Plato. *Timaeus, Critias, Cleitophon, Menexenus, Epistles.* Translated by R. G. Bury. Cambridge, MA: Harvard University Press, 1929.

Rexine, J. E. "Atlantis: Fact or Fantasy." *Classical Bulletin* 51 (1974–1975): 49–53.

Rodriguez-Ramirez, A., Enrique Flores-Hurtado, Carmen Conrerasm, et al. "The Role of Neo-tectonics in the Sedimentary Infilling and Geomorphological Evolution of the Guadalquivir Estuary (Gulf of Cadiz, SW Spain) during the Holocene." *Geomorphology* 219, no. 15 (August 2014): 126–40.

Rodriguez-Ramirez, A., José Noel Pérez-Asencio, Ana Santos, et al. "Atlantic Extreme Wave Events during the Last Four Millennia in the Guadalquivir Estuary, SW Spain." *Quaternary Research* 83, no. 1 (January 2015): 24–40.

Ruiz, F., et al. "The Holocene Record of Tsunamis in the Southwestern Iberian Margin: Date and Consequences of the Next Tsunami." Universidad de Huelva, 2013. https://studylib.es/doc/5347082/the-holocene-record-of-tsunamis-in-the -southwestern-iberi. Accessed on June 20, 2020.

Schulten, A. *Ancient Geography and Ethnography of the Iberian Peninsula* [Spanish] Madrid, Spain: Consejo Superior de Investigaciones Cientificas, 1958.

———. "Atlantis" *Ampurias* 1 (1939): 33–53.

———. *Tartessos* [Spanish]. Second edition. Madrid, Spain: Espasa Calpe, 1945.

Stemman, R. *Atlantis and the Lost Lands.* Garden City, NY: Doubleday, 1977.

Sullivan, R. *Atlantis Rising: The True Story of a Submerged Land Yesterday and Today.* New York: Simon & Schuster, 1999.

Tsirkin, Juli B. "The Hebrew Bible and the Origin of Tartessian Power." *Aula Orientalis* 4 (1986): 179–85.

———. "The Phoenicians and the Tartessos," *Gerion,* no. 15 (1997): 15–25.

Vitaliano, D. B. "Atlantis: A Review Essay." *Journal of the Folklore Institute* 8 (1971): 68–76.

———. *Legends of the Earth: Their Geologic Origins.* Bloomington: Indiana University Press, 1973.

Wilson, Colin. *From Atlantis to the Sphinx.* New York: Fromm International, 1997.

Wilson, Colin, and Rand Flem-Ath. *The Atlantis Blueprint: Unlocking the Ancient Mysteries of a Long-Lost Civilization.* New York: Delacorte Press, 2001.

Wingate, R. *Lost Outpost of Atlantis.* New York: Everest House, 1980.

Zangger, E. *The Flood from Heaven: Deciphering the Atlantis Legend.* New York: William Morrow & Company, 1992.

Zink, David. *The Stones of Atlantis.* London: W.H. Allen, 1978.

CHAPTER 2: SEARCHING FOR ATLANTIS IN 2016

Books about Atlantis, Tartessus, and Egypt by Georgeos Díaz-Montexano can be found at http://goo.gl/hhPDuj.

Bonacker, W. "The Egyptian 'Book of the Two Ways.'" *Imago Mundi. A Review of Early Cartography* 7 (1950): 5–17.

Bucher, Paul. *Les textes des tombes de Thoutmosis III et d'Aménophis II.* Mémoires publiés par les membres de l'Institut français d'archéologie orientale. Vol. 40. Cairo: Institut français d'archéologie orientale, 1932.

Budge, E. A. Wallis. *The Egyptian Heaven and Hell: Vol. I. The Book of Am-Tuat.* Chicago: Open Court, 1906.

———. *The Book of the Dead: The Chapters of Coming Out by Day.* London: Kegan Paul, Trench Trübner & Co., 1898.

Clagett, Marshall. *Ancient Egyptian Science.* Vol. 1. Philadelphia: American Philosophical Society, 1989.

Collado Giraldo, Hipólito, Jose Julio García Arranz, Arturo Domínguez García, Aldecoa Quintana, María Amparo. *Corpus de Arte Rupestre en Extremadura.* Vol. 2. Mérida, Spain: Editora Regional de Extremadura 2007.

Faulkner, R. O. *The Ancient Egyptian Coffin Texts.* Liverpool, UK: Liverpool University Pres, 2004.

Desroches Noblecourt, Christiane. *Amours et fureurs de La Lointaine: Clés pour la compréhension de symboles égyptiens.* Paris: Stock/Pernoud, 1995.

Gessler-Löhr, B. "Reliefblock aus einem Grab in Saqqara." In *Skulptur—Malerei, Papyri und Särge,* edited by H. Beck, 139–53. Melsungen, Germany: Verlag Guttenberg, 1993.

Graefe, Erhart. "Untersuchungen zur Wortfamilie bj3-." PhD dissertation, Universität zu Köln, 1971.

Guilmant, Félix. *Le tombeau de Ramses IX.* Cairo: Imprimerie de Institut Français d'Archéologie Orientale du Caire.

Hays, H. M. "Transformation of Context: The Field of Rushes in the Old and Middle Kingdom Mortuary Literature." In *D'un monde à l'autre: Textes des pyramides et textes des sarcophages.* Actes de la table ronde internationale "Textes des Pyramides versus Textes des Sarcophages," IFAO, September 24–26, 2001. Cairo: Institute Français d'Archéologie Orientale.

Hornung, Erik. *Das Amduat: Die Schrift des Verborgenen Raumes.* Ägyptologische Abhandlungen 7, 13, in 3 Parts (Wiesbaden: Harrassowitz, 1963, 1967).

Hummel, S. "Vignette zum ägyptischen Totenbuch, Kap.110." *Orientalia Suecana* 31–32 (1982–1983): 43–45.

Leclant, J. "Earu-Gefilde." In *Lexikon der Ägyptologie 1,* edited by W. Helck and E. Otto 1156–60. Wiesbaden: Harrassowitz, 1975.

Lefébvre, Eugéne. *Les hypogées royaux de Thèbes.* Mission archéologique française au Caire: Mémoires, Vols. 2–3, fasc. 1–2. Paris: E. Leroux, 1886–89.

Lesko, L. "The Field of Hetep in Egyptian Coffin Texts," *JARCE* 9 (1971–72): 89–101.

Loret, Victor. "Le champ des souchets." In *Recueil de travaux relatifs à la philologie et archéologie: Égyptiens et Assyriens.* Paris: Emile Bouillon, 1890.

Maspero, Gaston. "Les hypogées royaux de Thèbes." In *Études de mythologie et d'archéologie égyptienne*, Vol. 2. Paris: E. Leroux, 1893.

Maystre, Charles. "Le tombeau de Ramses II." *Bulletin de l'Institut Français d'Archéologie Orientale du Caire* 38 (1939) : 183–90.

Molinero Polo, M. A. "La cartografía egipcia del Más Allá en los libros funerarios del Reino Medio," In *Realidad y Mito*, ed. F. Diez de Velasco, M. Martínez and A. Tejera, 173–201. Madrid: La Laguna, 1997.

Munro, P. "Brothälften und Schilfblätter." *Göttinger Miszellen* (1973): 13–16.

Naville, È. *Das Todtenbuch der Ägypter I.* Berlín: Reed. 1971.

Piankoff, Alexandre. "Les deux papyrus 'mithologiques' de Her-Ouben au Musée du Caire." *Annales du Service des Antiquités de l'Égypte* 49 (1949).

———. Les grandes compositions religieuses dans la tombe de Pedemenope. *Bulletin de l'Institut Français d'Archéologie Orientale du Caire* 46 (1947).

———. *The Tomb of Ramesses VI: Egyptian Religious Texts and Representations* Bollingen Series 40, 2 vols. New York: Pantheon, 1954.

Pierret, Paul. *Recueil d'inscriptions inédites du Musée Égyptien du Louvre*. Vol. 1. Étude égyptologiques. Paris: Librarie Franck, 1874.

Porter, Bertha, and Rosalind L. B. Moss. *Topographical Bibliography of Ancient Egyptian Hieroglyphic, Text, Reliefs, and Paintings: Vol. 1 The Theban Necropolis, Part II: Royal Tombs and Smaller Cemeteries.* Oxford: Oxford University Press, 1989.

Renouf, P. Le Page (trans.). *The Book of the Dead.* London: Society of Biblical Archaeology, 1895.

Roulin, G. "Les tombes royales de Tanis: Analyse du programme décoratif." In *Tanis: Travaux récents sur le Tell Sân el-Hagar. Mission Française des fouilles de Tanis 1987– 1997*, edited by Phillipe Brissaud and Christiane Zivie-Coche. Paris: Noêsis, 1998.

Weill, Raymond. *Le champ des roseaux et le champ des offrandes dans la religion funéraire et la religion générale.* París: Guethner, 1938.

CHAPTER 3: DEAD SEA SCROLLS AGAIN

Aharoni, Y. "The Expedition to the Judean Desert, 1960, Expedition B." *Israel Exploration Journal* 11(1961):11–24, pls. 4–11C.———. "The Expedition to the Judean Desert, 1961, Expedition B—The Cave of Horror." *Israel Exploration Journal* 12 (1962): 186–99, pls. 23–34.

Allegro, J. M. *The Chosen People: A Study of Jewish History from the Time of the Exile until the Revolt of Bar Kocheba (Sixth Century B.C. to Second Century A.D.).* Garden City, NY: Doubleday, 1972.

———. *The Dead Sea Scrolls: A Reappraisal.* Second edition. Harmondsworth, UK: Penguin, 1977.

———. *The Dead Sea Scrolls and the Christian Myth.* London: Westbridge Books, 1979.

———. *Search in the Desert.* London: W. H. Allen, 1965.

———. *The Treasury of the Copper Scroll: The Opening and Decipherment of the Most Mysterious of the Dead Sea Scrolls, a Unique Inventory of Buried Treasure.* Garden City, NY: Doubleday, 1960.

———. *The Treasury of the Copper Scroll* Second revised edition. New York: Doubleday, 1964.

———. "An Unpublished Fragment of Essene Halakha (4Q Ordinances)." *Journal of Semitic Studies* 6 (1961): 71–73.

Avi-Yonah, M., N. Avigad, N, Y. Aharoni, I. Dunayevsky, and S. Gutman. "The Archaeological Survey of Masada, 1955–1956." Israel Exploration Journal 7, no. 1 (1957): 1–60.

Bar-Adon, P., "The Expedition to the Judean Desert, 1960, Expedition C." *Israel Exploration Journal* 11 (1961): 25–35, pls. 11D–17A.

Cross, F. M., Jr. *The Ancient Library of Qumran and Modern Biblical Studies: The Haskell Lecture, 1956–1957.* Third edition. Minneapolis: Fortress, 1995.

———. "Excursus on the Paleographical Dating of the Copper Document." In *Discoveries in the Judean Desert of Jordan III: "Les Petites Grottes" de Qumran* by M. Baillet, J. T. Milik, and R. de Vaux, 217–21. Oxford: Oxford University Press, 1962.

———. "The Manuscripts of the Dead Sea Caves," *Biblical Archaeologist* 17 (1954): 2–21 (the first page has a photograph of the two copper rolls in situ).

Cross, F. M., Jr., and D. N. Freedman. *Early Hebrew Orthography: A Study of the Epigraphic Evidence*, New Haven, CT: American Oriental Society, 1952.

Cross, F. M., Jr., and J. T. Milik. "Explorations in the Judaean Buqe'ah," *Bulletin of the American Schools of Oriental Research* 142 (1956): 15–17.

de Vaux, R. *Archaeology and the Dead Sea Scrolls: The Schweich Lectures of the British Academy.* 1959 rev. English edition. London: Oxford University Press, 1973.

———. "Exploration de la region de Qumran (Les Rouleaux de Cuivre), *Revue Biblique*, 60 (1953) : 55758.

———. "Manuscrits de Qumran (Le trésor du Rouleau de Cuivre, J.M. Allegro)," *Revue Biblique* 68 (1961): 146–47.

———. "Preface" and "Introduction." In *Discoveries in the Judean Desert of Jordan III: Les Petites Grottes*, 200–202. Oxford: Oxford University Press, 1962.

Benoit, P., J. T. Milik, R. de Vaux *Discoveries in the Judean Desert II, Les Grottes de Murabba'at*, Oxford: Clarendon, 1961.

Bailet, M., J. T. Milik, and R. de Vaux, with H. W. Baker. *Discoveries in the Judean Desert of Jordan III, Les "Petites Grottes" de Qumran.* Oxford: Clarendon, 1962.

Eck, W. "The Bar Kokhba Revolt: The Roman Point of View." *Journal of Roman Studies* 89 (1999): 76–89.

Eliav, Y. Z. "Hadrians Actions in the Jerusalem Temple Mount according to Cassius Dio and Xiphilini Manus." *Jewish Studies Quarterly* 4 (1997): 125–44.

Eshel, H., Magen Broshi, Richard Freund, and Brian Schultz. "New Data on the Cemetery of Khirbet Qumran." *Dead Sea Discoveries* 9, no. 2 (2002): 125–85.

Finkelstein, L. "Rabbi Akiba, Rabbi Ishmael, and the Bar Kokhba Rebellion." In *Approaches to Ancient Judaism*. Vol. 1, edited by J. Neusner, 3–10. Atlanta, GA: Scholars Press, 1990.

Fitzmyer, J. A. "Bargil Pixner, 'Archaologische Beobachtungen zum Jerusalemer Essener-Viertel und zur Urgemeinde,' *Christen und Christliches in Qumran?*, 89–113." *Old Testament Abstracts 16* (1993): 575.

———. "Dead Sea Scrolls," *NCE* 4, 676a–81a.

———. *The Dead Sea Scrolls: Major Publications and Tools for Study, With an "Addendum."* Missoula, MT: Society of Biblical Literature – Scholars Press, 1977.

———. "*The Treasure of the Copper Scroll* by John Marco Allegro." *Theological Studies* 22 (1961): 292–96.

Fitzmyer, J. A., and D. J. Harrington. *A Manual of Palestinian Aramaic Text (Second Century B.C. – Second Century A.D.)*. Biblica et Orientalia 34. Rome: Biblical Institute, 1978.

Flint, Peter W. "5/6HevNumbers" and "5/6HevPsalms." In *Miscellaneous Texts from the Judaean Desert*, edited by James R. Charlesworth et al., 137–66. DJD 38. Oxford: Clarendon Press.

Freund, R. "The Cave of Letters Excavations." [Hebrew] *National Geographic* (Israel 2001), 52–59.

———. *Digging through History*. Lanham, MD: Rowman & Littlefield, 2012.

———. *Digging through the Bible*. Lanham, MD: Rowman & Littlefield, 2008.

———. "A New Interpretation of the Incense Shovels of the Cave of the Letters." In *The Dead Sea Scrolls: Fifty Years after Their Discovery*, Jerusalem Congress, July 20–25, 1997, 644–60. Jerusalem: Israel Exploration Society in Cooperation with the Shrine of the Book, Israel Museum, 2000.

———. *Secrets of the Cave of Letters*. New York: Paragon, 2005.

Freund, R., and R. Arav. "An Incense Shovel from Bethsaida." *Biblical Archaeology Review* 23, no. 1 (January–February 1997): 32.

Freund, R., Philip Reeder, Harry Jol, and Carl Savage. *Dead Sea: New Discoveries in the Cave of Letters*. New York: Peter Lang, 2018.

Lapperrousaz, E-M. "L'etablissement de Qoumran pres de la mer Morte: Forteresse ou couvent? (avec evocation du 'Rouleau de cuivre'; 3Q15)," *Eretz Israel: Archaeological, Historical and Geographical Studies* 20 (1989): 118–23.

———. "Methodologie et datation des manuscrits de lay Mer Morte: Le Rouleau du cuivre, 3Q15." In *New Qumran Text und Studies: Proceedings of the First Meeting of the International Organization for Qumran Studies, Paris, 1992*, edited by George J. Brooke and Florentino Garcia Martinez, 233–39. Leiden: Brill, 1994.

———. *Qoumran: L'etablissment essenien des bords de la Mer Morte: Histoire et archeologie du suite*. Paris: Picard, 1976.

Lehmann, M. *Essays and Journeys* [Hebrew]. Jerusalem: Mosad Harav Kok, 1982.

———. "Identification of the Copper Scroll Based on its Technical Terms." *Romische Quartalschrift fur Christliche Alterumskunde und Kirchengeschichte* 5 (1964): 97–105.

———. "A New Interpretation of the Term 'Shadmoth.'" *VT* 3 (1953): 361–71.

———. "On My Mind." *Algemeiner Journal: A National Jewish Journal* Friday, April 30, 1993.

———. "Where the Temple Tax Was Buried: The Key to Understanding the Cooper Scroll," *Biblical Archaeological Review* 19 (1993): 38–43.

McCarter, P. K. Jr. "The Copper Scroll Treasure as an Accumulation of Religious Offerings." In *Methods of Investigation of the Dead Sea Scrolls and the Khirbet Qumran Site: Present Realities and Future Prospects*, edited by Michael Owen Wise, Norman Golb, John J. Collins, and Dennis G. Pardee, 133–48. New York: New York Academy of Sciences, 1994.

———. "The Mysterious Copper Scroll: Clues to Hidden Temple Treasure?" *Biblical Research* 8 (1992): 34–41, 63–64.

———. "The Mystery of the Copper Scroll." In *The Dead Sea Scrolls after Forty Years*. Symposium at the Smithsonian Institution, October 27, 1990, 40–55. Washington, DC: Biblical Archaeology Society, 1991.

———. "The Mystery of the Copper Scroll." In *Understanding the Dead Sea Scrolls: A Reader from the Biblical Archaeology Review*, edited by Hershel Shanks, 227–41. New York: Random House, 1992.

Pixner, B. "Copper Scroll (3Q15)." In *Anchor Bible Dictionary*, edited by David Noel Freedman, 1:1133a–1134a. New Haven, CT: Yale University Press.

———. "Das Essenquartier in Jerusalem und dessen Einfluss auf die Urkirche." *Das herilige Land* 113 (1981): 3–14.

———. *An Essene Quarter on Mount Zion?* Studia Hierosolymitana, Part 1: Archaelogical Studies, Collectio Maior 22, Studium Biblicum Franciscanum. Jerusalem: Francisca Printing, 1976.

———. Unravelling the Copper Scroll Code: A Study of the Topography of 3Q15." *Revue de Qumran* 11 (1983–85) 323–67.

Schechter, S. *Documents of Jewish Sectaries, Volume 1: Fragments of a Zadokite Work*. New York: Ktav, 1970.

Schultz, B. "The Qumran Cemetery: 150 Years of Research." *Dead Sea Discoveries* 13, no. 2 (2006)" 194–228.

Wolters, Albert M. "Apocalyptic and the Copper Scroll." *Journal of Near Eastern Studies* 49 (1900): 145–54.

———. "The Copper Scroll." In *The Dead Sea Scrolls after Fifty Years: A Comprehensive Assessment*, edited by. Peter W. Flint and James C. VanderKam, 1:302–23. Leiden: E. J. Brill, 1998.

———. *The Copper Scroll: Overview, Text and Translation*. Sheffield, UK: Sheffield Academic Press, 1996.

———. "The Copper Scroll and the Vocabulary of Mishnaic Hebrew." *Romische Quartalschrift fur Christliche Alterumskunde und Kirchengeschichte* 14 (1990): 483–95.

———. "The Fifth Cache of the Copper Scroll: 'The Plastered Cistern of Manos.'" *Romische Quartalschrift Fur Christliche Alterumskunde Und Kirchengeschichte* 13 (1988): 167–76.

———. "History and the Copper Scroll," *ANYAS* 722 (1994): 285–98.

———. "The Last Treasure of the Copper Scroll," *Journal of Biblical Literature* 107 (1988): 419–29.

———. "Literary Analysis and the Copper Scroll." In *Intertestamental Essays in Honour of Jozef Tadeusz Milik, Part 1*, edited by Zdislaw J. Kapera, 239–52. Krakow, Poland: Enigma, 1992.

———. "Notes on the Copper Scroll (3Q15)." *Romische Quartalschrift Fur Christliche Alterumskunde Und Kirchengeschichte*12 (1987): 589–96.

———. "The Shekinah in the Copper Scroll: A New Reading of 3Q15 12.10," In *The Scrolls and the Scriptures: Quman Fifty Years After, Journal for the Study of the Pseudepigrapha*, Supplement Series 26i, edited by Stanley E. Porter and Craig A. Evans, 382–92. London: Roehampton Institute, London Papers 3, 1997.

Zeitlin, Solomon, "The Dead Sea Scrolls: 1. The Lamech Scroll—A Medieval Midrash. 2. The Copper Scrolls. 3. Was Kando the Owner of the Scrolls?" *Jewish Quarterly Review* New Series 47 (1956/57), 245–68.

CHAPTER 4: ARCHAEOLOGY OF JEWISH RESISTANCE

Arad, Yitzhak. *Belzec, Sobibor, Treblinka: The Operation Reinhard Death Camps*. Bloomington: Indiana University Press, 1987.

Bauer, Yehuda. *Rethinking the Holocaust*. New Haven, CT: Yale University Press, 2001.

Bauman, P., B. Hansen, Y. Haimi, I. Gilead, R. Freund, P. Reeder, M. Bem, and W. Mazurek. "Geophysical Exploration of the Former Extermination Center at Sobibor, Poland." 23rd EEGS Symposium on the Application of Geophysics to Engineering and Environmental Problems, Annual Meeting, Session on Urban and Archaeological Geophysics, April 8–11, 2010.

Blatt, Thomas Toivi. *From the Ashes of Sobibor*. Evanston, IL: Northwestern University Press, 1997.

Browning Christopher. *The Origins of the Final Solution: The Evolution of Nazi Jewish Policy, September 1939–March 1942*. Lincoln: University of Nebraska Press, 2004.

———. *Remembering Survival: Inside a Nazi Slave Labor Camp*. New York: W. W. Norton, 2010.

Dawidowicz, Lucy S., ed. *The Golden Tradition: Jewish Life and Thought in Eastern Europe*. New York: Holt, Rinehart and Winston, 1967.

———. *The War Against the Jews, 1933–1945*. New York: Bantam, 1976.

Engelking, Barbara, and Jacek Leociak. *The Warsaw Ghetto: A Guide to the Perished City* (New Haven, CT: Yale University Press, 2009.

Freund, Richard. *Archaeology of the Holocaust: Vilna, Rhodes, and Escape Tunnels*. Lanham, MD: Rowman & Littlefield, 2019.

———. *Digging through History: Religion and Archaeology from Atlantis to the Holocaust*. Lanham, MD: Rowman & Littlefield, 2012.

Gilead, I., Yoram Haimi, and Wojciech Mazurek, "Excavating Nazi Extermination Centres." *Present Pasts: Journal of the Institute of Archaeology Heritages* 1, no. 1 (2009): 10–39.

Grossman, Vasily, and Ilya Ehrenburg. *The Black Book: The Ruthless Murder of Jews by German-Fascist Invaders Throughout the Temporarily-Occupied Regions of the Soviet Union and in the Death Camps of Poland during the War 1941–1945* [English from the Russian]. London: Holocaust Library, 1986.

Gutman, Israel. *The Jews of Warsaw, 1939–1943: Ghetto, Underground, Revolt.* Bloomington: Indiana University Press, 1982.

Hilberg, Raul. *The Destruction of the European Jews.* New Haven: Yale University Press, 2003.

———. *The Warsaw Diary of Adam Czerniakow: Prelude to Doom.* Chicago: Ivan R. Dee, 1999.

Kaplan, Chaim A. *Scroll of Agony: The Warsaw Diary of Chaim A. Kaplan.* Bloomington: Indiana University Press, 1999.

Kassow, Samuel. *Who Will Write Our History? Emanuel Ringelblum, the Warsaw Ghetto, and the Oyneg Shabes Archive.* Bloomington: Indiana University Press, 2007.

Kola, Andrzej. *Bełżec: The Nazi Camp for Jews in the Light of Archaeological Sources—Excavations 1997–1999.* Washington, DC: United States Holocaust Museum, 2000.

Langer, Lawrence. *The Holocaust and the Literary Imagination.* New Haven, CT: Yale University Press, 1977.

———. *Holocaust Testimonies: The Ruins of Memory.* New Haven, CT: Yale University Press, 1991.

Mosse, George L. *The Crisis of German Ideology: Intellectual Origins of the Third Reich.* New York: Schocken, 1981.

———. *Toward the Final Solution: A History of European Racism.* New York: Howard Fertig, 1978.

O'Neil, Robin. "Belzec-The 'Forgotten' Death Camp." *East European Jewish Affairs* 28, no. 2 (1998): 49–62.

Parkes, James. *Anti-Semitism.* Chicago: Quadrangle Books, 1969.

Pechersky, Sasha. "The Sobibor Uprising." In *Sefer Milchamot HaGetaot* [Hebrew], edited by Itzchak Tzukerman and Moshe Bassok, 539–56. Kibbutz HaMeuchad, Israel, 1954).

Rashke, Richard. *Dear Esther.* Lincoln, NE: Morris Publishing, 2000.

———. *Escape from Sobibor.* Urbana: University of Illinois Press, 1995.

Roiter, Howard, and Kalmen Wewryk. *To Sobibor and Back: An Eyewitness Account.* Volume 1. Montreal: Concordia University Chair in Canadian Jewish Studies and the Montreal Institute for Genocide and Human Rights, 1999.

Weinberg, Gerhard. "The Final Solution and the War in 1943." In *Revolt Amid the Darkness.* Washington, DC: United States Holocaust Memorial Museum, 1993.

Willenberg, Samuel. *Surviving Treblinka.* Oxford: Blackwell, 1989.

Zuckerman, Yitzchak. *A Surplus of Memory: Chronicle of the Warsaw Ghetto Uprising.* Berkeley: University of California Press, 1993.

Index

About the Author

Dr. Richard A. Freund was the Bertram and Gladys Aaron Professor of Jewish Studies at Christopher Newport University and directed over forty different archaeological projects in Israel, Lithuania, Latvia, Poland, Spain, Cyprus, and Greece with a team of geoscientists and local archaeologists. The work of his team has been featured in thousands of media outlets worldwide and in twenty-five television documentaries. Dr. Freund was the author of over one hundred scholarly articles and author or coauthor of fourteen books, including *The Archaeology of the Holocaust: Vilna, Rhodes, and Escape Tunnels* (Rowman & Littlefield, 2019).

LONGWOOD PUBLIC LIBRARY
800 Middle Country Road
Middle Island, NY 11953
(631) 924-6400
longwoodlibrary.org

LIBRARY HOURS

Monday-Friday	9:30 a.m. - 9:00 p.m.
Saturday	9:30 a.m. - 5:00 p.m.
Sunday (Sept-June)	1:00 p.m. - 5:00 p.m.